CRICUT PROJECT IDEAS

37 ORIGINAL CRICUT PROJECT FROM BEGINNERS TO EXPERT TO START CREATING AND EARNING WITH AMAZING OBJECTS, RIGHT NOW!

EMILY TYLER

© Copyright 2020 - All rights reserved.

The content contained within this book may not be reproduced, duplicated or transmitted without direct written permission from the author or the publisher.

Under no circumstances will any blame or legal responsibility be held against the publisher, or author, for any damages, reparation, or monetary loss due to the information contained within this book. Either directly or indirectly.

Legal Notice:

This book is copyright protected. This book is only for personal use. You cannot amend, distribute, sell, use, quote or paraphrase any part, or the content within this book, without the consent of the author or publisher.

Disclaimer Notice:

Please note the information contained within this document is for educational and entertainment purposes only. All effort has been executed to present accurate, up to date, and reliable, complete information. No warranties of any kind are declared or implied. Readers acknowledge that the author is not engaging in the rendering of legal, financial, medical or professional advice. The content within this book has been derived from various sources. Please consult a licensed professional before attempting any techniques outlined in this book.

By reading this document, the reader agrees that under no circumstances is the author responsible for any losses, direct or indirect, which are incurred as a result of the use of information contained within this document, including, but not limited to, errors, omissions, or inaccuracies.

TABLE OF CONTENTS

INTRODUCTION 6

CHAPTER 2: HOW TO USE A CRICUT MACHINE? 10
- Cricut Machine 15
- Cricut Working 16
- Types of Cricut machines 17
- Cricut Can Be Used To Cut Materials 18
- Which Cricut Accessories & Supplies Do I Need? 19
- Where To Find Materials 26

CHAPTER 3: WHAT CAN THE CRICUT DO? 28
1. A Coloring Flowering Card Page Project with Cricut 28
2. Recipe Stickers 30
3. Wedding Invitations 33
4. Custom Pads 35
5. Crepe Paper Bouquet 37
6. Southwest Cacti 39
7. Leaf Banner 42
8. Paper Pinwheels 44

CHAPTER 4: EASY CRICUT PROJECTS 46
9. Wall Decoration 46
10. Customize You Snack Bag 50
11. Creative Herbarium 53
12. Fabric Pennant 56
13. Paperbox 59

CHAPTER 5: PROJECTS FOR BEGINNERS 62
14. Wedding Table Plan 62
15. Paper Decoration 67
16. Crepe Paper Flowers 73
17. Floral Letter In Watercolor 81
18. Paper Fans 86
19. Thankyou Box 88

CHAPTER 6: PROJECTS FOR CONNOISSEURS OR "INTERMEDIATE" 92
20. Fabric Headband 92
21. Forever Fabric Banner 95
22. Fabric Flower Brooch 97

23	Leather Flower Hat	99
24	Floral Mousepad	101
25	Jelly Bean Burp Cloth	103
26	Personalized Coaster Tiles	105

CHAPTER 7: PROJECTS FOR EXPERTS 108

27	Personalized Mugs (Iron-On Vinyl)	108
28	Personalized Coaster Tiles	111
29	Vinyl Chalkboard	114
30	Glitter Tumbler	116
31	Personalized Mermaid Bottle	120
32	Gift Wrap	123

CHAPTER 8: SPECIAL OCCASION PROJECTS 126

33	Halloween Spiders	126
34	3-in-1 Winter Crafts Snowflake	128
35	Spiderweb Garland	131
36	Christmas Ornament	133
37	Wedding Invitation	136

CHAPTER 9: HOW TO SELL YOUR PROJECT ONLINE 140

All About Copyright 141
Cricut Angel Policy 142
Starting A Cricut Craft Business 143
How To Set The Price 144
Monetizing Your Art 145
Approaching Local Markets 154

CHAPTER 10: IMPORTANT TIPS & TRICKS TO KNOW WHEN YOU WANT TO SELL YOUR OWN CREATIONS 156

Would You Market Cricut Layouts? 156
What Are the Most Lucrative Cricut Companies? 156
Could I Sell Cricut Pictures On Etsy? 157
What Can I Create To Market Using A Cricut Maker? 157
Private use vs. Industrial use 158
Licensed Pictures 159
Beginning A Cricut Craft Business 159
Narrow Your Own Cricut Craft Niche 159
Purchase Materials In Bulk 161

CONCLUSION 162

Introduction

Past people used to have some different methods for maintaining memories. The caveman's days had impressions imprinted onto the walls as carvings and sketches. The guy of the 15th century has identical approaches combined with working in their diaries and journals.

The techniques became more refined and simpler to implement, as the years passed. Fast forward into the next century and events have phenomenally progressed.

You glance about with a clenched hand, and the laws of science. You still have too many resources in place that will help you retain the unique memories of time, like the video camera. The optical speech recorder and the camcorder.

Wouldn't you know life is good? We do have another resource that has assisted people tremendously with their scrapbooking demands. This is Cricut.

Ultimately Cricut has amazing features to improve your imagination as a novice or as a specialist. As a true matter.

This computer, even though you are not that imaginative in real life, will make you come across as a master model.

It's a perfect way to be a skilled crafter and find a device or partner that allows you the opportunity and pursue your passion. Happily, Cricut has created an awesome tool with advanced cutting technologies for everyone who wants to go in crafts that will aid you cut, build and carry all the beautiful art ideas of yours to life.

Knowing what devices and accessories that can be used with the Cricut to minimize your time for preparation and save you headaches. Very versatile is the circuit and can be utilized to connect at any point in the project with several forms of materials. This book is for beginners and contains advanced Cricut projects as well, where you can discover everything you need to know about what the Cricut machine of yours and how to bring the best out of your device. Well, show all the confidential information that will enable you to use your device in no time like a specialist!

If you love to sculpt a Cricut machine-particularly with paper and vinyl-is a good investment. It will make your cut designs appear clean and polished, and your crafts would be far easier to build until you're comfortable in using it. There are several forms you can earn money for your Cricut, such as online or at art fairs selling personalized t-shirts, mugs, decals, etc. The main aim for this Cricut book writing is to help you become a full pro of Cricut machine by the time you finish reading and also to start implementing your projects immediately.

It is in the spirit of dedicated and creative DIYers to explore the world of crafts and strive towards coming up with new designs and interesting new techniques as well as trying out new tools to make the best out of your crafting time. It appears that Cricut machines are getting more popular in the domain of crafting miracles, which is no wonder since Cricut machines offer a variety of possibilities that are not limited to cutting various types of materials. Aside from enabling easy cutting of a great variety of materials, Cricut machines offer additional functions, such as embossment, drawing, and folding, depending on which machine you are using for your crafts and projects.

If you have never worked with a Cricut machine before, or if you are only starting to work with Cricut, we recommend starting your journey from the first part of the book, consider yourself a beginner in the world of Cricut crafting.

We are going to present you with different types of Cricut machines and features available at your disposal with each one of the available models. One thing is for certain - you are in for a true crafting delight with endless possibilities that the knowledge in Cricut brings. We will also present you with some basic project suggestions you can start with as you are being introduced with functions of Cricut machines. As you are progressing further with your Cricut techniques and crafting skills, you will be able to continue with learning more about Cricut designs and crafts through the next part of the book reserved for Advanced Cricut Makers. Start with the first part of the book and begin learning everything you need to know about Cricut tools, materials, and projects. Useful tips and techniques for Cricut projects are only pages away so dive in!

CHAPTER 1:

How to Use A Cricut Machine?

O ne should not forget that the cool thing about Cricut is that projects are endless. You might decide to have your own wall lettering, or you might choose to make a nursery at home, and you would need to make that distinct wall painting with several letters. Instead of you spending several hours cutting with blades and carving with knives or any other cutting device, you just need a Cricut machine. You do not even need to hire a muralist for your hand painting because you can do that yourself. In fact, people like these are happy that you are not exposed to this knowledge so that they can make some cash from you. The die-cut machine produces those precise cuts which children and other professional needs. There are several die-cut stickers you can get from this machine. This machine also allows you to render wedding favors and party favors quickly by helping in the creating process of tags, bags, boxes, and several other party creations. These pieces can come in several forms like gift bags, banners, hats, etc. These and many more can fit the theme of any party because you are making them. As much as someone would love to shy away from the scrapbook stuff one just cannot. Now, just picture your daughter or your son getting married and you present him/her with a scrapbook having pictures from the very first day they stepped into this planet to where they are now. Gifts like this sound odd, but they are invaluable because you are not giving out a utensil or a tool you are giving out those memories. Scrapbooks carry out many memories and those feelings you cannot give through your regular gifts.

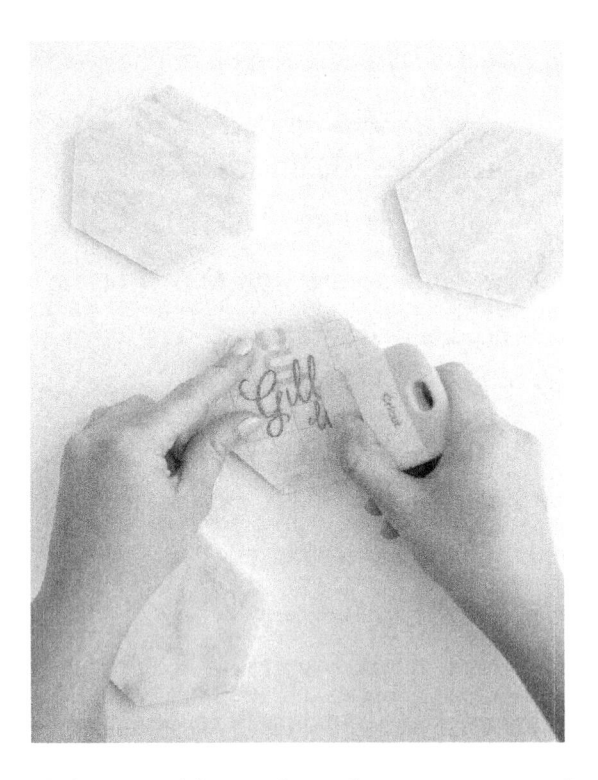

If you have a Cricut machine and you have not gotten these supplies, we advise that you get them as soon as possible. We are aware that these supplies are grouped into different categories.

We should not forget that the vinyl is another material which you need to make your work on the Cricut machine smooth. The Cricut machine can work on those delicate materials which can be used to make decals, stencils, graphics, and those beautiful signs too. You can cut through the following vinyl materials, chalkboard vinyl, dry erase vinyl, holographic vinyl, stencil vinyl, printable vinyl, matte vinyl, adhesive vinyl, printable vinyl, and glossy vinyl also. Furthermore, you may have so much experience in the fabric and textile world, and you want to infuse the Cricut machine. Some of the materials or fabrics that you can work with are; canvas, denim, cotton fabric, linen, leather, flannel, burlap, duck cloth, felt, metallic leather, polyester, printable materials, silk, wool felt and many more others. If you have not got your iron-on vinyl. Which is meant to be the heat transfer vinyl. You make use of this vinyl to decorate a t-shirt, tote bags and other kind of fabric items that you can think of like; printable iron-on, glitter iron-on, glossy iron-on, flocked iron-on, holographic sparkle iron-on, metallic iron-on, neon iron-on, foil iron-on, etc.

We should not narrow our minds to the materials mentioned above because there are several other materials which the Cricut can cut through or even work on some of them include; adhesive wood, corkboard, balsa wood, craft foam, aluminum sheets, corrugated paper, embossable foil, foil acetate, paint chips, plastic packaging, metallic vellum, printable sticker paper, stencil material, shrink plastic, wrapping paper, window cling, wood veneer, washi tape, birchwood, wrapping paper, wood veneer, plastic packaging, soda can, glitter foam, printable magnet sheets, etc. The Cricut maker can work on materials which are up to 2.4mm thick and other unique materials and distinctive fabrics like the; jersey, cashmere, chiffon, terry cloth, tweed, velvet, jute, knits, moleskin, fleece, and several others.

This machine can be found anywhere and everywhere, so much paper artwork is done. What this suggests is that you can see these machines in schools, offices, craft shops, etc. You can make use of this Cricut machine for a school project, card stock projects as well as iron-on projects too. Making use of this machine to cut out window clings is not a bad idea at all. It is not limited to this because you also engage in projects that have to do with adhesive stencil and stencil vinyl also. You would remove the stencil vinyl after it is dried. This would leave a distinct imprint. You can also make use of this machine to create lovely fashion accessories like several pieces of jewelry. The Cricut machine allows you to make use of the faux leather for exceptional designs. Recall that we talked about school projects. Preschoolers and their instructors can benefit from this machine. Furthermore, you can print out photos or images from your computer while making use of this machine, especially from the printable magnets to those sticker papers, customized gifts, bags, etc.

Defining objects requires you to use other similar purposes to drive home your point and to give the reader a clearer picture. The very possible way we can describe a Cricut machine is to say that it is a machine that has so much resemblance with the printer, but it is used majorly for cutting designed pieces. That is a straightforward and easy definition you do not need to bother yourself about that. Just picture a printer in your mind and think of a cutting device. If you already have the Cricut machine with you. You would notice that it uses precise blades and several templates or rollers during cutting.

Against what people think. The machine is not meant for scrapbook keepers or makers alone. I still do not know why this idea has become so much rooted in the minds of people that we have grown to allow this thought to dominate our reactions and attitude towards any new innovation.

The world has been transformed with that machine as its products have been able to add those unique visual beauties to the simple paperwork that we know. The Cricut machine has several models and versions some of them include Cricut Expression, Expression 2, Cricut Imagine, Cricut Gypsy, Cricut Cake Mini, Cricut Personal Cutter, Cricut Crafts Edition and Martha Stewart and the Cricut Explore Air. The tool obviously fits into any type of craft you are working on. And there is also a die-cut machine which gives you that extra-precise, sharp, and smart cutting. The process of cutting materials by hand during crafts has been reduced drastically. Thanks to this beautiful machine. More also, you can perform multiple projects all at the same time due to the effectiveness of this device. It contains several cartridges which are always available to help you explore different forms and shapes of several designs. More also that move from one project to another has been made possible with the use of this Cricut machine. Any material can be shaped into that design you want it to be. Furthermore, you can also create patterns which are already pre-installed in the software that comes with it. The design software tool becomes very much available with pre-loaded designs for instant use. We are sure you must have been able to purchase this machine from your local craft store on the online store. You are aware that the price was based on the kind of model you are using and we are sure that you've been able to narrow down your needs for you to be able to get your machine because anything which makes your work easier and faster is a significant investment and the Cricut machine is definitely one. Due to the efficiency of this machine, we now have it in several places we never thought. We have them in offices and specific workshops. If you feel that the Cricut is a home-only tool, you are entirely wrong. This time-saving device allows your work to be very professional, and the beautiful thing about it is that we have no limits to what it can do. We are sure that you are reading this to gain more ideas and you hastily want to jump into making things and doing some stuff. Yes, that is cool; however, we need to understand some basics else we would be making serious mistakes, or the process would look very confusing.

Cricut Machine

Cutting machine is a Cricut that can be used for different projects of crafting. It takes projects that you make or submit into their software of design space and cuts them. It sounds easy but we guarantee you'll be surprised by how many things you can do in very less time you'd be willing to accomplish it by hand. We're talking about sewing patterns, calendar stamps, for home wooden labels, mugs monogrammed, and a lot of different things.

This device is great for the imaginative individual who still needs to do projects like DIY but has a limited time to wait on the page of your Pinterest. Also, whether you've got a home-built company or Etsy store, we will pretty much make sure you get much profit from the device.

Cricut Working

You can wirelessly connect this machine to your laptop, build or export designs to your laptop, and submit them for cutting to the Cricut. Cricut has design space software (available for MAC

Windows, and smartphone) that let you in creating and importing cutting designs with your computer. Inside the Cricut, there is a small blade (or scoring tool, or pen, or rotary cutter).

Once a material you have that is ready to be cut in the Design Space, add the desired material to a 12" wide cutting pad, transfer your design wirelessly from the computer or laptop to the Cricut, and then the material is loaded in your machine.

Your project should begin cutting with a click of a button.

Types of Cricut machines

In the market, three forms of the Cricut machines are there currently. Cricut Joy (this one just came out), Cricut Maker, and Cricut Explore Air II. Choosing which device, you need to purchase would rely on the kind of project you choose to create.

All devices come with the free software Design Space.

<u>Explore Air 2 Cricut</u>

For most projects, the device is this we would consider purchasing. It is the most common machine from Cricut, and it can cover most of the materials you can need for a broad range of projects DIY such as vinyl, cardstock, paper, and chipboard.

With this device, you can cut more than 100 items, and use 4 methods to hack, compose, and score.

Cricut Maker

Cricut maker unit performs all the Explore Air 2 Cricut can do, like cutting heavier or more fragile items such as leather, fabrics, and thin woods.

With this unit, more than 300 items can be cut, and use more than 12 devices for cutting, scoring, writing, and other effects pro-level. If you decide to delve into more complex ventures and play with a broader variety of products, we will suggest this machine.

Cricut Joy

Cricut Joy, the new Cricut machine, is a further compact machine for simple, daily DIY projects, then the other machines. Materials can be cut up to 5.5" wide only but long material (around 20 feet) you can buy.

More than 50 items it cuts and can utilize two tools for writing and cutting. If you would like to invest less and for simple projects creation like vinyl posters, cards and little iron-on patterns, we will suggest this tool.

Cricut Can Be Used To Cut Materials

Everyone likes to think of these Cricut machines like vinyl or cutting paper, but the fact is that much stuff can be cut with the Cricut. The Explore Air 2 Cricut will potentially break over 60 styles of materials.

Some Cricut machines will cut materials like silk, leather and even wood as well as paper, vinyl & cardstock.

You'll want to switch to the blade deep-cut for better cut consistency with thicker materials.

And with 100x the Explore Air 2 's pressure capacity, the latest Cricut Maker will cut further materials also (100 +). Are you looking for specialty?

This has a completely latest rotary blade due to which it is a necessity for seamstresses, who can now plan a job in minutes rather than hours.

Which Cricut Accessories & Supplies Do I Need?

All Cricut machines come with everything you need to begin cutting already in the box.

The essential fine-point edge, cutting mats, and all the force strings you need are included.

The one thing that isn't included is material to cut.

The main question you have to ask yourself is, "What kind of projects do I want to do with my machine?"

Different activities require different cutting materials (like paper, vinyl, wood.). However, they may require extra tools and embellishments to be able to be cut by your machine.

Here is my definitive rundown of Cricut accessories and supplies for beginners, plus a couple of things that aren't essential, though you might find them useful for later.

Must-Have Cricut Supplies and Materials

The supplies and materials you need to begin with your Cricut differ a ton, depending upon the kinds of projects you like to do. That makes it somewhat difficult to propose "unquestionable requirements" as far as materials go. However, I do have three unique materials I figure everybody should have a go for cutting at any rate, to make sure you can get the hang of your machine and check whether you like those kinds of projects!

Vinyl

The first is vinyl. Glue vinyl comes in an assortment of styles, like matte, lustrous, sparkle, foil, holographic, open-air, rushed, dry erase, and writing slate. The sky is the limit from there. It tends to be used for anything, from decals and names to customized kitchen compartments, electronic devices covers, vehicle windows — whatever your heart wants.

For individuals starting at the beginning, I recommend getting the Cricut vinyl sampler, which has twelve 12"×12" sheets of glue vinyl that come in a variety of colors. (There's a metallics vinyl sampler as well, if you need to attempt some fun metallics for your project!) That will kick you off.

Iron-On

The following thing I propose to everyone is heat transfer vinyl or iron-on. Once more, iron-on comes in huge amounts of colors and styles, like to matte, reflective, sparkle, foil, adaptable, designed, neon, and others. It's incredible for tweaking T-shirts, baby onesies, caps, group or clubwear, packs, covers, home décor, and more!

My preferred activity with iron-on is to make baby onesies. They are so easy to make, and they are the ideal present for any new mother! I recommend getting an Everyday Iron-On Sampler Pack to begin; every sampler pack has three 12"×12" sheets of iron-on in a variety of matching colors.

Paper

The third material I think everyone should attempt is paper! Even if you don't do a great deal of papermaking, it's constantly enjoyable to make personalized greeting cards and envelopes! There is a huge variety of types of paper, including designed scrapbook papers, cardstocks, blurb boards, foil or sparkle papers, ridged cardboards, kraft papers, and more.

I think everybody should get a cardstock sampler in whatever colors they like best.

Fabric

If you have a Cricut Maker, you should get some fabric and take a stab at cutting it (even if you don't do a ton of sewing or fabric projects regularly)! You can go to your neighborhood fabric store and get anything you desire, as the sharp rotational edge can cut through most fabrics like butter. They even have fusible fabric — so cut, iron, and go!

"Nice-to-Haves" You Can Splurge On Later

After you've gotten the essential accessories and supplies and have begun to get gradually better with your machine, you may feel ready to take on more advanced types of projects. Here are some of my most-loved Cricut supplies and extras! You don't necessarily need these, but if you're using your machine constantly and loving it, these are amazing to have!

Storage

When you start using your machine to an ever-increasing extent, you're going to begin accumulating more tools and materials! Cricut has adorable specialty travel totes that are ideal for putting away tools and extras. They also make machine totes to organize what is intended to securely store or move your machine, along with all the extra strings and adornments. Furthermore, the machine tote can slide over the handle of the moving tote and stack directly on top for simple transportation of both simultaneously!

Specialty Materials

In the "must-have supplies" list, the most fundamental materials are vinyl, iron-on, and paper. But there are TONS of specialty materials that are great to use in your activities! Here is a list of my top picks and what I use them for:

Vinyl

- Basic – Comes in matte, reflective, metallic, and so forth.

- Premium Outdoor/Permanent – Comes in matte, gleaming, metallic, pearl, and more. For any outside projects or activities that may get wet (vehicle window decals, mugs, tumblers, and so on).

- Premium Removable – For any task in which you need to remove and/or throw away the vinyl later (holiday window clings, for example). (Quick note: this vinyl is removable for as long as two years after you initially apply it. However, it can't be reused. If you don't end up removing it, it will essentially function as basic vinyl.)

- Patterned – Comes with printed structures on the vinyl itself. Use it anywhere you'd use basic or removable vinyl.

- Sparkle, Holographic, and Adhesive Foil – Comes in heaps of gleaming, sparkly colors. Use it wherever you'd use basic or removable vinyl, but want to add some gleam, shimmer, and sparkle.

- Stencil – Clear, glue-backed vinyl that is ideal for making your stencils to use on wood, canvas, paper, plastics, and more!

Iron-On

- Basic – Comes in matte, shiny, and metallic. Works incredibly well on the most available variety of base materials, including wood, and can be layered! In general, iron-on projects include shirts, tote bags, onesies, caps, home decorations, frills, and so forth.

- Foil, Holographic, and Glitter – For any project you would use everyday iron-ons for, but that you want to add some gleam, shimmer, and sparkle to.

- Patterned – Comes with printed designs on the iron-on itself. Use anyplace you'd use everyday iron-ons.

- SportsFlex – Thin, lightweight iron-on that stretches and flexes. Ideal for iron-on projects on activewear and tech fabrics like polyester and nylon.

Paper

- Scrapbook – Comes in every shading and pattern possible. For most paper ventures, including cards, scrapbook pages, party decorations, and so forth.

- Foil Embossed, Pearl, and Sparkle/Shimmer – For any paper venture for which you would use Scrapbook paper.

- Cardstock – Comes in a vast array of colors and sparkle alternatives too. For most paper projects (greeting cards, school projects, event decorations, and so forth).

- Posterboard – Comes in many different colors and foil hues. For projects where you need a thicker, increasingly solid paper (blessing boxes, school projects, standards, and so on).

Maker-Only Materials

If you have a Cricut Maker, there are some additional materials that this model of Cricut can cut!

- Chipboard – Super strong board for projects that need a great deal of help (gift boxes, photograph outlines, labels)

- Leather – Both genuine leather and faux leather for leather projects (satchels, belts, hair bows).

- Felt – Medium-weight felt for any felt project (children's artworks, infant accessories, stuffed shapes).

- Corrugated cardboard – Comes with planning level sheets and corrugated ones. For projects in which you need to include size or surface (3D projects, designs, children's artworks, cards, scrapbooking).

- Kraft Board – Sturdy, substantial weight paper that doesn't break, tear, or leave white score marks.

  For any paper project in which you need some additional strength (gift boxes, packs, photo frames, tags, banners).

Other Fun Materials

- Foil acetate – A clear material ideal for card overlays, frames, gift boxes, envelopes, stylistic themes, and so on.

- Party foil – Medium-weight reflective foil sheets for party decor.

- Window cling – Make static cling decals in any shape or size. Good for holidays, special events and parties, child's exercises, and school projects.

- Washi tape – Low-tack, semi-opaque adhesive perfect for layering with paper.

- Printable materials – Great for making your own vinyl and stickers.

Where To Find Materials

One of the exciting parts of Cricut Design Space is that the materials are not hard to find; they are all around you. There are online stores where you can easily get the materials you want. Although different e-stores have varying prices, the point is to get the ideal quality.

There are four popular online stores where Cricut machine users, both beginners, and professionals, get materials for their Cricut projects, and they are; Cricut.com, Amazon, Joann, and Michaels. These stores provide almost every supply and bundle you'll be needing. They have the materials, tools, and accessories, and even the Cricut machines needed. Feel free to visit each store and compare their prices before purchasing.

Also, you can look around for stores in your local area where sell the most common types of materials that can be used on Cricut machines, mostly paper products.

At this stage, we have been able to cover most of the basics of Cricut machines, materials, tools, and accessories. You should now know their functionalities and purposes to some extent. It's high time we proceeded to the technical and complex part of making use of Cricut for different designs and crafts. From here onward, we will not discuss much the properties of Cricut machines, materials, tools, or accessories. It will be majorly about how you can set up your Cricut machine and what you can do with it. We're getting to the interesting parts.

If you need to upgrade your Cricut machines, buy any material, tool, or accessory, you should make plans for that now. The more resources you have, the more you can explore.

CHAPTER 2:

What Can The Cricut Do?

1 A Coloring Flowering Card Page Project with Cricut

Pick your most loved cardstock hues and prepare to make a card that is hand-hued and loaded with affection. If you need to give an additional uncommon card and blessing, leave the card un-shaded and include incorporate with certain markers or watercolor pencils (I would adore those shading endowments!). Tip: Keep the plan similarly as seems to be, move things around or include your very own touch... you make the structure to shading! This likewise makes an extraordinary card for Mother's day.

Materials

- Cricut Explore air 2 and Floral Coloring Card Make-it-now project
- Cricut Design Space programming
- Flower cutouts and heart accessories structured.
- 12" x 12" StandardGrip Cricut® tangle
- Cardstock and paperwhite
- Black Cricut pen (.03 or 12 PM, fine point size)
- Colored pencils and markers – discretionary

Materials to make your own shading card with your Cricut machine

Instructions

- Follow directions to draw and cut the blossom shading card plan in Cricut Design Space.
- Fold the card along the scoreline. Shading anyway you'd like.
- Fold score lines and paste side folds inside the back of an envelope.
- Add confetti inside envelope, seal and send.

2 Recipe Stickers

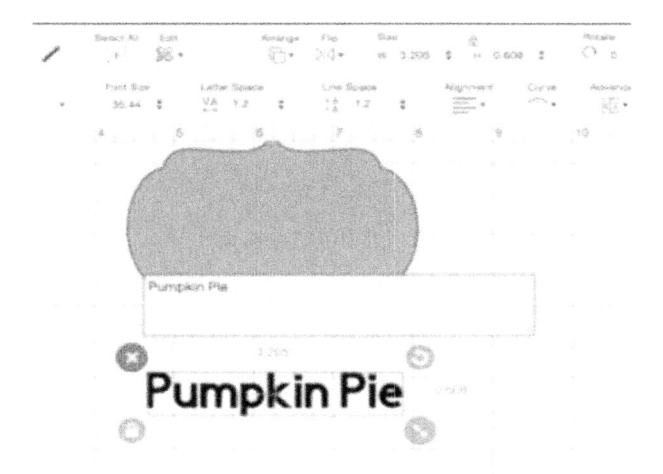

Materials

- "Cricut Maker" or "Cricut Explore"
- sticker paper
- cutting mat

Instructions

- Log into the "Design Space" application and click on the "New Project" button on the top right corner of the screen to view a blank canvas.

- Click on the "Images" icon on the "Design Panel" and type in "stickers" in the search bar. Click on desired image, then click on the "Insert Images" button at the bottom of the screen.

- The selected image will be displayed on the canvas and can be edited using applicable tools from the "Edit Image Bar". You can make multiple changes to the image as you need, for example, you could change the color of the image or change its size (sticker should be between 2-4 inches wide). The image selected for this project has words "stickers" inside the design, so let's delete that by first clicking on the "Ungroup" button and selecting the "Stickers" layer and clicking on the red "x" button. Click on the "Text" button and type in the name of your recipe, as shown in the picture below.

- Drag and drop the text in the middle of the design and select the entire design. Now, click on "Align" and select "Center Horizontally" and "Center Vertically".

- Select the entire design and click on "Group" icon on the top right of the screen under "Layers panel". Now, copy and paste the designs and update the text for all your recipes.

Tip: Use your keyboard shortcut "Ctrl + C" and "Ctrl + V" to copy and paste the design.

- Click on "Save" at the top right corner of the screen to name and save your project.

- To cut your design, just click on the "Make It" button on the top right corner of the screen. Load the sticker paper to your

"Cricut" machine and click "Continue" at the bottom right corner of the screen to start cutting your design.

- Note – The "Continue" button will only appear after you have purchased images and fonts that are available for purchase only.

- Set your cut setting to "Vinyl" (recommended for sticker paper since it tends to be thicker than regular paper). Place the sticker paper on top of the cutting mat and follow the prompts on the screen to finish cutting your design. Viola! You have your own customized recipe stickers.

3 Wedding Invitations

Materials

- "Cricut Maker" or "Cricut Explore"

- cutting mat and Cardstock or your choice of decorative paper/ crepe paper/ fabric

- home printer (if not using "Cricut Maker")

Instructions

- Log into the "Design Space" application and click on the "New Project" button on the top right corner of the screen to view a blank canvas.

- Let's customize an already existing project by clicking on the "Projects" icon on the "Design Panel" and selecting

"Cards" from the "All Categories" drop-down then type in "wedding invite" in the search bar.

- For example, you could select the project shown in the picture below and click "Customize" at the bottom of the screen to edit and personalize the text of your invite.

- Click "Text" on the "Designs Panel" and type in the details of the invite. You can change the font, color and alignment of the text from the "Edit Text Bar" on top of the screen and remember to change the "Fill" to "Print" on the top of the screen.

- Select all the elements of the design and click on "Group" icon on the top right of the screen under "Layers panel". Then, click on "Save" to save your project

- Your design can now be printed and cut. Click on "Make It" button and follow the prompts on the screen first to cut the printed design.

4 Custom Pads

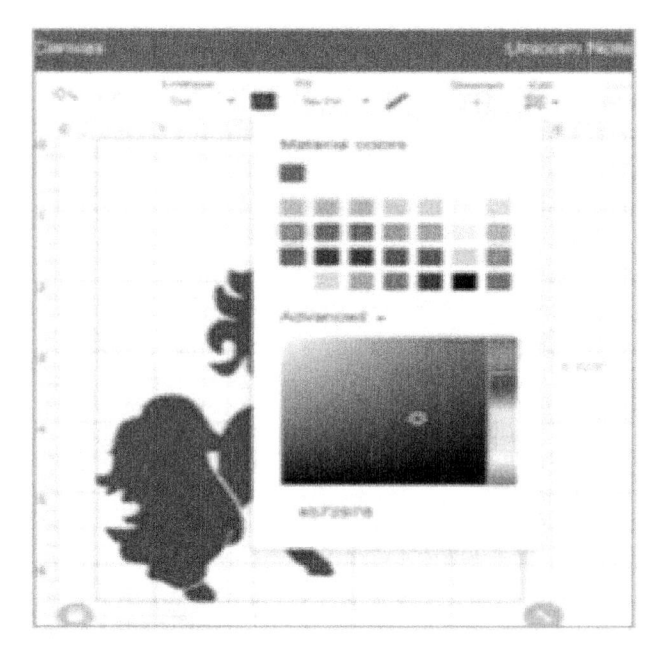

Materials

- "Cricut Maker" or "Cricut Explore"

- cutting mat

- washi sheets or your choice of decorative paper/ crepe paper/ fabric.

Instructions

- Log into the "Design Space" application and click on the "New Project" button on the top right corner of the screen to view a blank canvas.

- Using an already existing project from the "Cricut" library and customize it. So click on the "Projects" icon on the "Design Panel" and type in "pad" in the search bar.

- Click on "Customize" so you can further edit the project to your preference. For example, the "unicorn pad" project shown below. You can click on the "Linetype Swatch" to change the color of the design.

- The design is ready to be cut. Simply click on the "Make It" button and load the washi paper sheet to your "Cricut" machine and follow the instructions on the screen to cut your project.

5 Crepe Paper Bouquet

Materials

- Cricut Maker" or "Cricut Explore"

- standard grip mat

- crepe paper in desired colors

- floral wire

- floral tape

- hot glue

- fern fronds

- vase

Instructions

- Log into the "Design Space" application and click on the "New Project" button on the top right corner of the screen to view a blank canvas.

- Let's use an already existing project from the "Cricut" library and customize it. So click on the "Projects" icon and type in "crepe bouquet" in the search bar.

- Click on "Customize" so you can further edit the project to your preference or simply click on the "Make It" button and load the crepe paper to your "Cricut" machine and follow the instructions on the screen to cut your project.

- To assemble the design, follow the assembly instructions provided under the "Assemble" unit of the project details.

6 Southwest Cacti

Desert flora plants appear to be the structure extra nowadays, yet imagine a scenario in which your home doesn't get full daylight. Make your own large paper desert plants to bring home a touch of Southwest style. These three-dimensional models can be set into basic earthenware pots, painted to coordinate your own stylistic layout. Reward: no untidy earth to manage!

Here, as well, are four straightforward structures that we slice with vinyl to tweak smooth stone liners. Include your own imaginative touch by finding various approaches to utilize these adorable prickly plant layouts.

Materials

- PAPER

- Art paper or enormous card stock paper

- banner board
- low-temp heated glue firearm
- paper twisting device
- shower mount or paste
- 12 × 24-inch cutting mat
- painted pot
- cutting-machine vinyl
- vinyl move material
- scissors
- weeding device
- shining device
- liners

Instructions

1. Cut pieces from card stock and one bit of base from banner board.

2. Overlap enormous bits of prickly plants along score lines.

3. With twisting device, delicately shape two layers of petals of prickly plants blossom.

4. With low-temp craft glue firearm, place spot on back of one petal layer and secure it onto focal point of second petal layer with the two sets twisting upwards.

5. Use splash mount or paste to append banner board and card stock base.

6. Slide tabs of huge desert plants piece into cuts on base, leaving two base cuts in the middle.

7. Rehash with second coordinating piece.

8. Slide the following piece with cut at base over other two.

9. Press tab into base on right side.

10. Rehash with conclusive tab to frame assemblage of prickly plant.

11. Add heated glue to definite little top-cut piece.

12. Join little top-cut piece to top of desert flora.

13. Slide different pieces into cut and paste set up.

14. Paste blossom to top of prickly plant.

15. Spot into painted pot

7 Leaf Banner

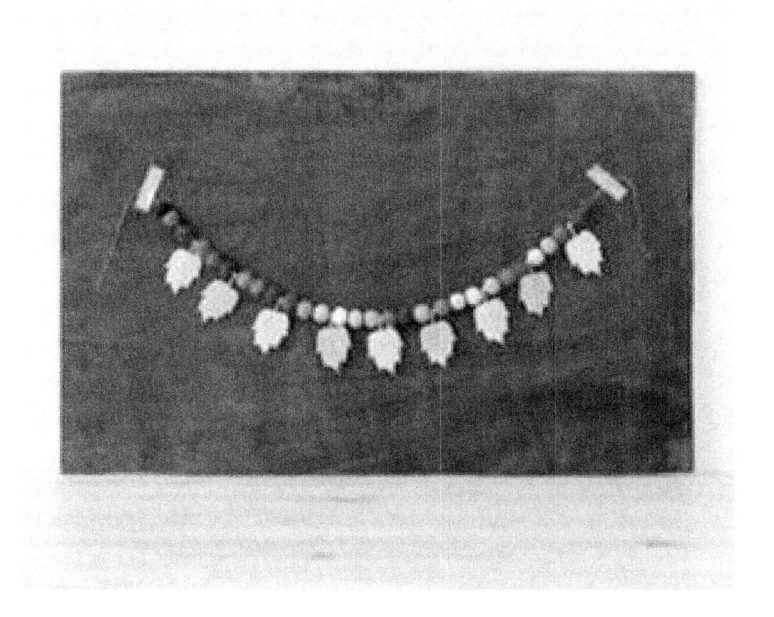

Materials

- "Cricut Maker" or "Cricut Explore"

- standardgrip mat

- watercolor paper and paint

- felt balls

- needle and thread

- hot glue

Instructions

- Log into the "Design Space" application and click on the "New Project" button on the top right corner of the screen to view a blank canvas.

- Let's use an already existing project from the "Cricut" library and customize it. So click on the "Projects" icon and type in "leaf banner" in the search bar.

- Click on "Customize" so you can further edit the project to your preference or simply click on the "Make It" button and load the watercolor paper to your "Cricut" machine and follow the instructions on the screen to cut your project.

- Use watercolors to paint the leaves and let them dry completely. Then create a garland using the needle and thread through the felt balls and sticking the leaves to the garland with hot glue, as shown in the picture below.

8 Paper Pinwheels

Materials

- "Cricut Maker" or "Cricut Explore"
- standardgrip mat
- patterned cardstock in desired colors
- embellishments
- paper straws
- hot glue

Instructions

- Log into the "Design Space" application and click on the "New Project" button on the top right corner of the screen to view a blank canvas.

- Let's use an already existing project from the "Cricut" library and customize it. So click on the "Projects" icon and type in "paper pinwheel" in the search bar.

- Click on "Customize" to edit the project to your preference further or simply click on the "Make It" button and load the cardstock to your "Cricut" machine and follow the instructions on the screen to cut your project.

- Using hot glue, adhere the pinwheels together to the paper straws and the embellishment, as shown in the picture below.

CHAPTER 3:

Easy Cricut Projects

9 Wall Decoration

Use a magnetic board to make a wall decoration in natural colors and organize your office things as well as possible.

<u>Materials</u>

- Magnetic canvas 30 x 40 cm and 6 extra strong magnets Ø 10 mm

- Natural cane 30 x 100 cm

- Round Cork plate 20 cm

- Pine frame 10x15 cm

- Acrylic multi-media - Matte White, matt fir green and gray mouse mat - 59 ml

- Wooden baguette

- Cricut Machine

- Imitation leather Kraft paper braiding tape - 9.5 cm

- Synthetic brushes flat n° 16 and round n° 4

- Paint roller

- Masking tape - 50m x 19mm - Monali

- A4 Cultura tracing paper

- B Monali graphite pencil

- Glue gun

- Templates to download

Instructions

1. Prepare the paint mixture with 1/3 green, 1/3 white and 1/3 gray.

2. Draw two parallel diagonals on the canvas and stick masking tape on each side, then paint in between.

3. Download and print the fern template and trace it onto a sheet of tracing paper. All this using Cricut machine.

4. Place the tracing paper upside down on the cork support and iron with a grease pencil on the lines in order to transfer the pattern.

5. Paint the pattern.

6. Disassemble the frame to keep only the wooden outline.

7. Cut a piece of cane the size of the frame and glue it to the front of the frame.

8. Glue 4 magnets to the 4 corners of the back of the frame.

9. Download and print the pocket template and cut the caning to get the same shape.

10. Glue strips of kraft on the 4 sides of the back of the caning to solidify it.

11. Glue a strip at the top, on the front, for the finish.

12. To form the pocket, fold and fold the bottom of the cane inwards, then the two sides.

13. Glue the whole with a dot of glue, where the bottom and sides meet.

14. Cut two 12 cm kraft strips. Fold them in half and glue the ends. Slide the wooden stick through the formed loops.

15. Snap the frame onto the magnetic canvas. Then place the other elements in order to visualize their location, then glue them with the glue gun.

16. The magnetic canvas is ready to decorate your desk.

10 Customize You Snack Bag

Now is the perfect time to personalize the snack bag (for your little ones and grown-ups!) With the Cricut cutting machine!

Materials

- a Cricut cutting machine (Cricut Maker , Cricut Explore Air2 or Cricut Joy)

- a snack bag - Maped

- iron- on adhesive in several colors. I chose black, white, gray, blue and red.

- Cricut EasyPress mini machine

- a cutting mat

- scissors (found in the Cricut precision tool set of 5)

- a stripping hook (found in the Cricut precision tool set of 5)

- a scraper

Instructions

1. On Design Space, prepare your project.

2. Start the cut by clicking on CREATE and follow the instructions. Select the Everyday IRON-ON material. Don't forget to click on mirror. Place the iron-on patch on your cutting mat, shiny side against the mat. Put the mat in the notches of the machine and press the buttons as requested on your screen.

3. When the cut is complete, unload the mat. Now, it's time for weeding.

4. With the weed hook, remove the material you do not need.

5. Without forgetting the small pieces inside the drawing.

6. Repeat the operation on all the cuts.

7. Before taking the break with the EasyPress mini, you need to prepare your media. For this you need: an Easy Press Mini, a terry towel, baking paper.

8. Now place the terry towel in the snack bag. Add a piece of parchment paper inside between the bag and the napkin.

9. Place the first layer of your project on the bag.

10. Cover with baking paper to protect the bag and apply the press (set to medium heat).

11. Gently peel off the plastic film from the iron-on patch.

12. Repeat with all the other cuts. To apply the design to the top of the bag, lay it flat on the napkin with baking paper in between.

13. Apply the text to the top of the bag. There you have it, you have personalized your child's snack bag!

11 Creative Herbarium

Learn how to dry your plants recovered in nature and collect them in your herbarium notebook or draw them in small drawing notebooks made yourself.

Materials

- Scandicraft Collection Herbarium Album
- Block of 24 assorted printed papers A4
- Assortment of 3 sheets of stickers
- Wooden press "My herbarium"
- Drawing pad A5 80 sheets - 90g - Monali
- A4 paper cutter
- Cricut maker
- Assortment of 3 washi tapes

- Fine black felt pen

- Double-sided adhesive tape - 6mm x 10m

- Sewing needle

- Sewing thread

- 1 pair of scissors

- Downloadable envelope and notebook templates

Instructions

1. Use of the press and the herbarium book 1. Collect fresh plants and flowers. Open the press to dry the plants. Take out the items: cardboard boxes, sheets of paper and foam.

2. Place a sheet of thin paper on cardboard. Position the plant to dry. Cut back the stem if necessary. Cover with a second sheet of thin paper. In addition to this, you need to know more about it.

3. Stack the cardboard boards on top of each other. Place in the press. Cover the last plant with a thin sheet and cardboard. Add the mousses. In addition to this, you need to know more about it.

4. Close the press on the plants. Screw as far as possible to crush the plants. Leave to dry for at least a week, especially for plants that are thick.

5. Gently remove the plants and flowers from the press. Open the herbarium notebook. Place the flowers and plants in the chosen location. Maintain with a piece of washi tape from the collection. Stick the rose with double-sided adhesive tape. Write the names of the plants. Stick a label to date the harvest and create a paper envelope to insert petals, seeds, etc.

6. Choose a paper from the collection. Fold in half crosswise. Measure 10.5 cm at the fold and cut with Cricut. Take 4 sheets of drawing paper. Fold them in half and cut them in the same way as for the blanket.

7. Mark the points to be drilled at the fold of the sheets using the template to download in Cricut. Pierce the leaves at the marks. Cut a sewing thread folded in 3. Pass the needle from the inside of the booklet to the cover. Bring the needle back to the center of the notebook and tie at the fold. Do the same for each pair of holes.

8. Cut the sheets that protrude from the notebook using the cutter. Decorate the cover with masking tape from the collection. Choose stickers and glue them in the center to finish decorating the cover. In addition to this, you need to know more about it.

9. Your notebooks are ready to be filled with pretty dried plants or drawn during your walks.

12 Fabric Pennant

The Cricut Maker machine gives you endless creative possibilities and one of the possibility is this fantastic project.

Materials

- The Cricut machine
- Nice cotton fabric!
- Tissue fusible golden - Discover the radius iron
- Fleece 100 x 100 cm Créalia - 150 g / m² - Créalia
- wooden rods

Instructions

For the first step, we start by cutting our fabrics with the Cricut machine to the desired shape. It is possible to use already existing templates or ideas via the CRICUT platform. For this DIY I decided to create my own shape for my banner. We therefore take care of cutting our formats to then mount our pennant and also cut the elements with the iron-on paper. For the banner, you must therefore create 2 patterns of the same format that will then be associated!

I decide to transfer my iron-on fabric to one side of my pennant. The great thing about this iron-on fabric is that we don't have to think about printing the design inside out. We only need an iron, a stable surface, a cloth or a very thin cloth to stick the element.

We start to assemble our pennant, we take our two pieces of fabric that we will come to associate. We start by sewing the top of the banner, then directly place the wooden rod which will serve as a support for hanging!

I wanted to give my pennant a little more volume, so I decided to integrate a fleece inside, which we cut to the approximate shape of our pennant. I cut here the fleece of a size relatively smaller than my fabric to have this filling effect and then in step 5 to be able to have enough room to come and sew all around!

I allow myself to put 3 small dots of glue to fix my fleece and be sure that it will not move afterwards!

We finish sewing all around our fabric to finally finish our pennant, everything is well hung. We can now add our little string and hang our pretty banner wherever you want!

13 Paperbox

This little word is very simple but it nevertheless has so much power ... Hidden in a box, you will be able to create a surprise and offer a THANK YOU full of love and tenderness to one of your loved ones or during a particular event.

Materials

- The Cricut Joy Machine
- Color papers
- Glue
- Removable gold vinyl
- Gold Marker - Cricut Joy

- The template that you will find attached

- The typos used are Courier new and Adelaide (the latter is from Cricut)

- For those who can log into Cricut, here is the Design Space project link.

Instructions

1. Using your application prepare the cutting of your paper templates for your box, as well as the paper decorations (ex: foliage / flowers / hearts).

2. Using your application prepare the cutting of your paper templates for your box, as well as the paper decorations (e.g.: leaves / flowers / hearts).

3. Prepare to cut your heart stickers with your SMART VINYL REMOVABLE Gold paper which you will use to close your box.

4. Now that the paper templates are cut out, use your GOLD marker to create and draw your texts. You can choose to write whatever you want.

5. It's time to stick your papers on your cardboard box. The "Thank you" paper is to be placed inside the box on the upper part. Also place your plain pink paper template at the bottom of your box.

6. Now stick your paper with your text "Just for you" on the outside of the box.

7. Come and create your floral arrangement inside your box using strong glue, I decided to add a real craspedia to it so that I don't just have paper. Alternatively, you can add a branch of eucalyptus, or olive tree.

8. Once your interior decoration is finished, you can now close your box and seal it with your golden heart stickers. All you have to do is offer them.

CHAPTER 4:

Projects For Beginners

14 Wedding Table Plan

Completion time: more than 2 hours.

Difficulty: 1/3

Materials

- Cricut Machine

- 1 box of 25 Pollen sheets 210x297 mm 210g - Ivory

- Extra strong double-sided adhesive tape - 6mm x 10m

- High temperature glue gun

- White metal ring 25 cm

- Straight scissors 17 cm

- 1 natural kraft string

Instructions

- Using the Cricut, cut multiple sheets using the different shades of green card stock.

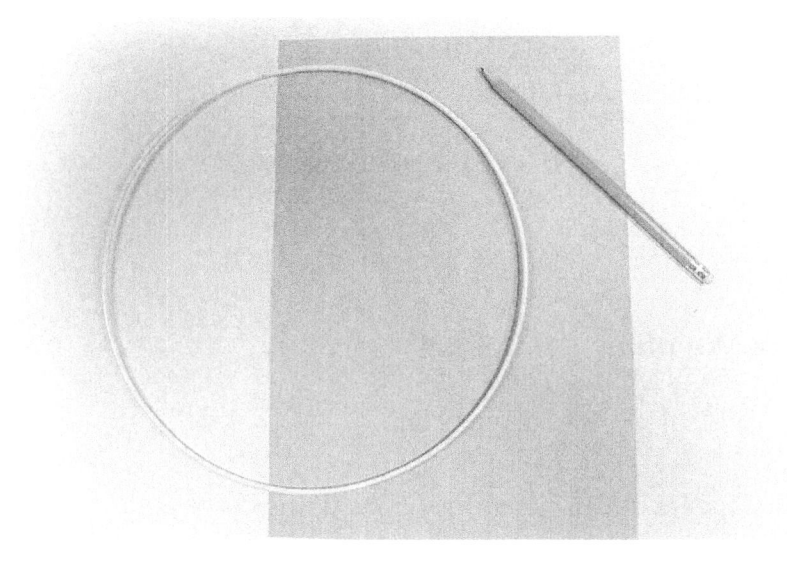

- Trace the inner and outer outline of the half of the ring on green card stock with a pencil, and cut out the half moon, leaving enough room on both sides to be able to fold it around the ring.

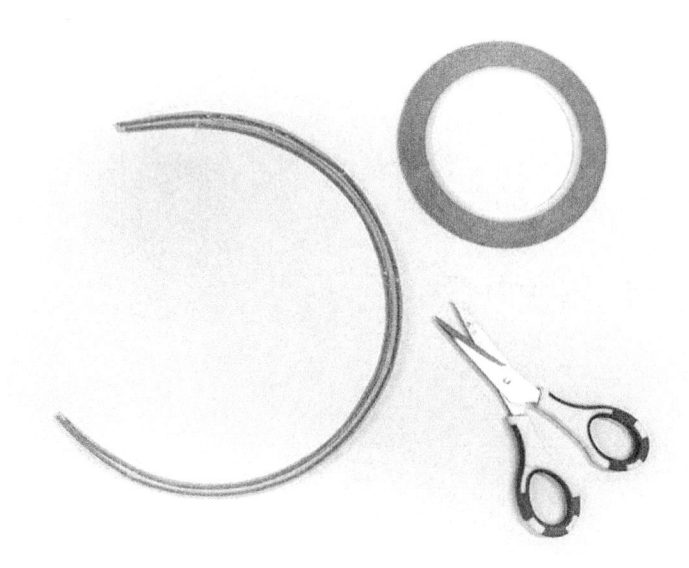

- Stick the double-sided adhesive tape on the half-moon.

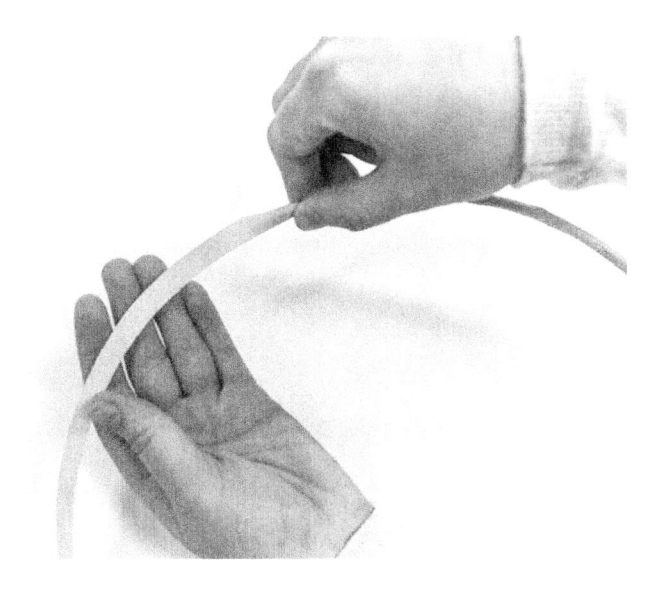

- Fold it around half of the hoop, pinching the edges so that they are secure. This edge will serve as a base for easily gluing your paper sheets.

- Arrange the different cut sheets on the part of the ring covered with paper and glue the elements with a glue gun.

- Using the Cricut and the Natural Leaves die, cut the berries out of the cream card stock.

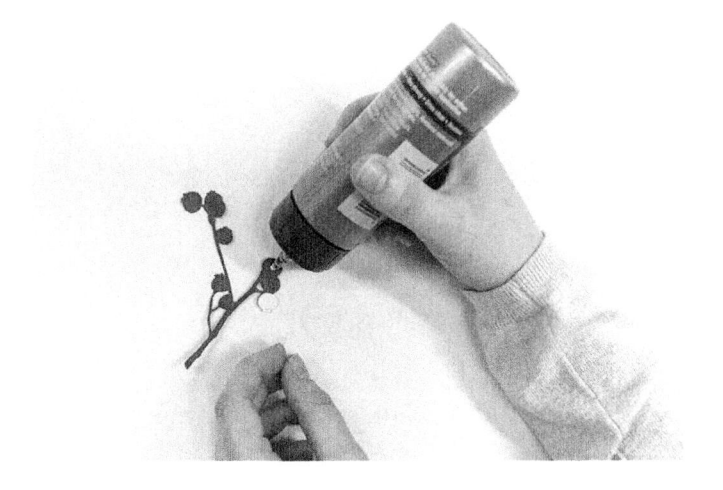

- Glue the berries on the corresponding branches of the set to bring out the berries.

- Insert and glue the berry branches among the other leaves where you want to add shades of color.

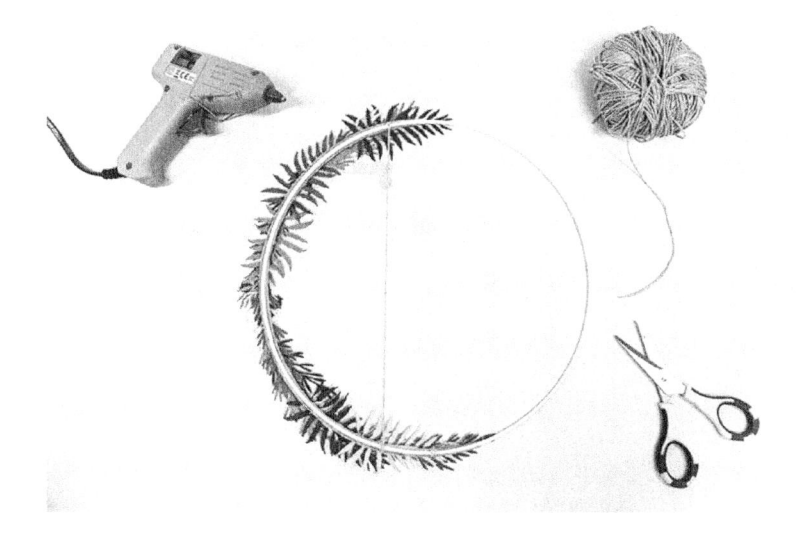

- Tie the string to the back of the metal ring with the glue gun, cut off the excess if necessary

- Print the table numbers on the cream card stock, cut out in a circle and glue it on the string, towards the center of the ring.

- Print the names of the guests on the cream paper and cut them out with scissors, forming banners.

- Create your seating plan and paste the guest names wherever you want!

- Create as many rings as there are guest tables for your wedding and arrange them on a recovered wooden pallet.

15 Paper Decoration

Materials

- Cricut

- Set of 6 Scrapbooking paper sheets -

- Leaf - 30.5x30.5cm - petrol blue .

- Leaf - 30.5x30.5cm - menthol green

- Leaf - 30.5x30.5cm - lime green

- Leaf - 30.5x30.5cm - spring green

- Slate scrapbooking sheet - 30x30cm

- Sheet of 34 epoxy stickers -

- 8 card stock polaroid frames -

- Assortment of 40 die-cuts -

- 100m two-tone spool - Sky blue

- 16 mini clothespins 35 mm

- Vivaldi smooth sheet A4 240g - Canson - white n ° 1

- Precision cutter and 3 blades

- Blue cutting mat - 2mm - A3

- Acrylic and aluminum ruler 30cm black

- Precision scissors 13.5cm blue bi-material rings

- 3D adhesive squares

- Mahé Tools - - scrapbooking

- Pack of 6 HB graphite pencils

Preparation time: 2h

Techniques: Stencil, Collage, Origami - Folding, Tropical

Instructions

Discover below all the steps to realize your summer decoration "Tropical Paradise":

- Gather the materials.

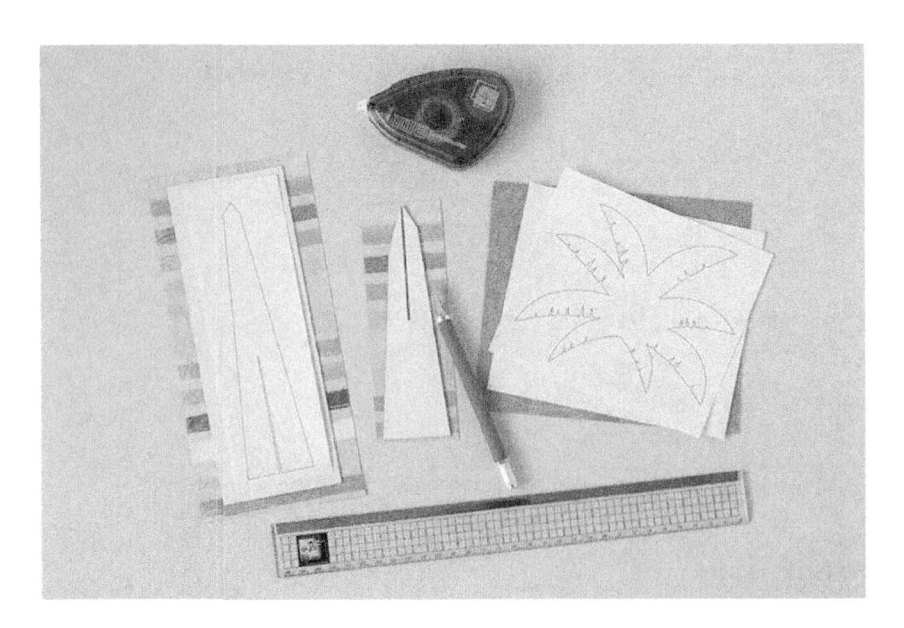

- Using the template and a pencil, reproduce the palm tree on the papers in the collection.

- Cut out using Cricut.

- Assemble the trunk of the palm tree. Glue the foliage. Using the template, reproduce the traces of the cocktail support on thin cardboard, following the dimensions indicated. Cover it with the collection paper.

- After having cut in the slate sheet: 1 x (8.5 x 8.5 cm). Choose a Polaroid. Glue the slate sheet to the back of the Polaroid. Using a chalk pen, write "Cocktail of the day". Decorate with the stickers. Fold the support at the dotted lines.

- Using the templates and a pencil, draw the leaves and flowers on the paper and on the collection paper. Draw.

- Choose photos. Cut them to size: 8.5 x 8.5 cm. Stick to the back of the Polaroids.

- Glue the leaves and flowers together. Cut the string to the desired dimensions and glue it to the back of the flowers. Glue the birds on the string and hang the photos using mini clips.

- And here is a pretty summer and tropical decoration! Beautiful evenings in perspective!

16 Crepe Paper Flowers

Completion time: more than 2 hours

Difficulty: 1/3

Materials

- Assortment of 10 rolls of crepe paper
- Or discover our range of crepe papers
- 20 thread stems with flower 1mm x 50 cm
- Vinyl glue
- 4 pairs of multi-use scissors
- Cutout template to download, print and cut.

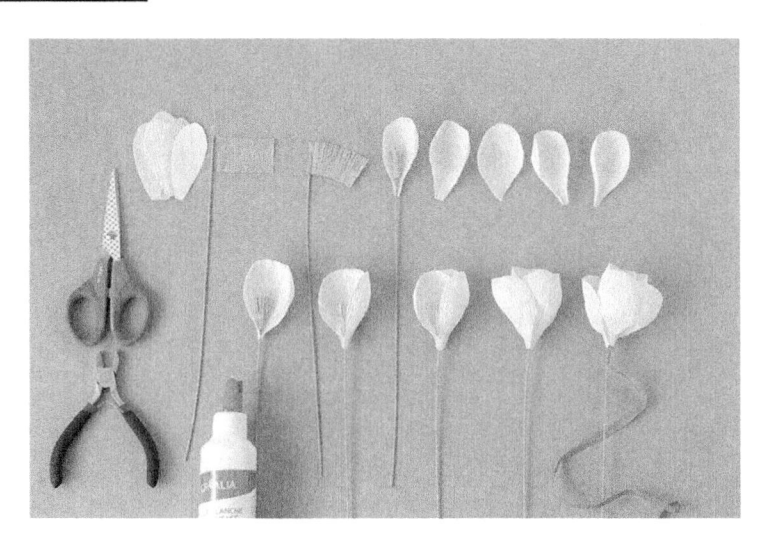

Instructions

Creation of yellow flowers:

Print the template and cut it out on Cricut. Cut 5 petals out of yellow florist crepe paper. Be sure to place the vertical template in the direction of the grooves of the crepe paper. Cut a 2.5 x 5 cm strip of orange florist crepe paper. Bisect a binding wire with a clamp cutting. Stretch each petal by placing your thumbs in the middle of the petals. Dig with your thumbs apart. The petals become very rounded. Finely notch the orange strip. Paste up the binding wire and winding the paper to form the pistils. Stick the pistils in the hollow of a first petal. Glue the second petal slightly offset by about 3mm. Glue all the petals until they half cover the first petal. Pinch the basis for refining. Cut a strip of green crepe paper about 0.5 x 15 cm long. Shoot it. Glue one end to the base of the petals. Apply glue and wrap it tightly around the rod. Leave to dry. Prepare 10 yellow flowers like this.

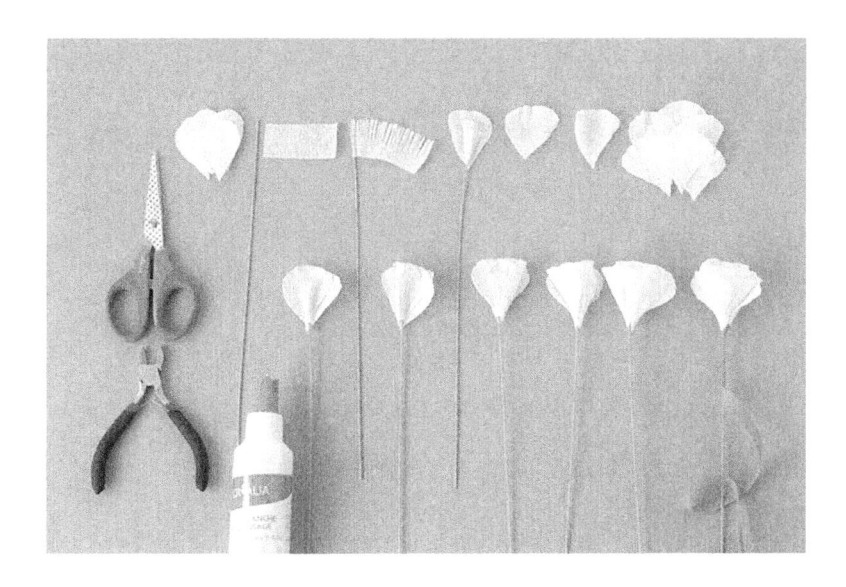

Creation of white

Cut 10 petals out of white florist crepe paper . Be sure to place the vertical template in the direction of the grooves of the crepe paper. Cut a 2.5 x 5 cm strip of yellow florist crepe paper.

Cut a wire to be tied in half using wire cutters.

Pinch the top edge of a petal starting from the left and spacing the inches 2 millimeters apart. Stretch the paper.

Move your thumbs and repeat the operation every 5 millimeters, to form little ruffles. Do the same for each petal. Place thumbs in the middle of the petals.

Dig lightly with your thumbs apart without completely stretching the paper.

Finely notch the yellow strip. Stick the top of the binding wire and winding the paper to form the pistils.

Stick the pistils in the hollow of a first petal. Glue the second petal offset by about 5 millimeters.

Glue all the petals by rolling the petals to surround the flower several times. Pinch the base to refine it.

Cut a strip of green crepe paper about 0.5 x 15 cm long. Shoot it. Glue one end to the base of the petals. Apply glue and wrap it tightly around the rod.

Let dry. Prepare and 10 white flowers.

Creating peony flowers:

Cut 7 petals of the first template out of bright pink florist crepe paper. Prepare 7 heart-shaped petals and 6 large petals and 5 sepals in green crepe paper . Sure to place the template vertical in the direction of paper grooves crepe.

Cut a 3.5 x 11 cm strip of orange florist crepe paper .

Cut into both a binding wire with a clamp cutting.

Stretch the orange strip. Fold it in 3 and cut.

Finely notch each orange strip . Glue the first strip to the top of the wire to be bound and roll up the paper to form the pistils.

Add the second, then the third strip. Spread the pistils to give them volume. Pinch the base to refine it.

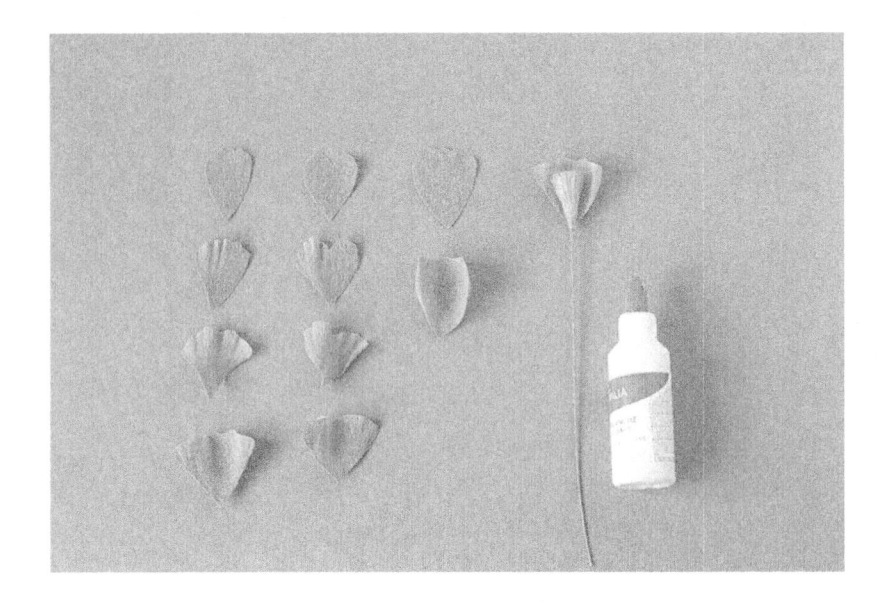

Give the form to the petals:

Take the first set of petals. Pinch the top edge of a petal starting from the left and spacing the inches 2 millimeters apart. Stretch the paper. Move your thumbs and repeat the operation every 5 millimeters, to form little ruffles. Do the same for each petal. Place thumbs in the middle of the petals. Widen slightly, keeping inch without fully extend the paper.

Prepare the same way the petals in a heart shape.

For larger petals, stretch them one by one. Place thumbs in the middle of the petals. Dig with your thumbs apart. The petals become very rounded.

Stick the pistils in the hollow of a first petal.

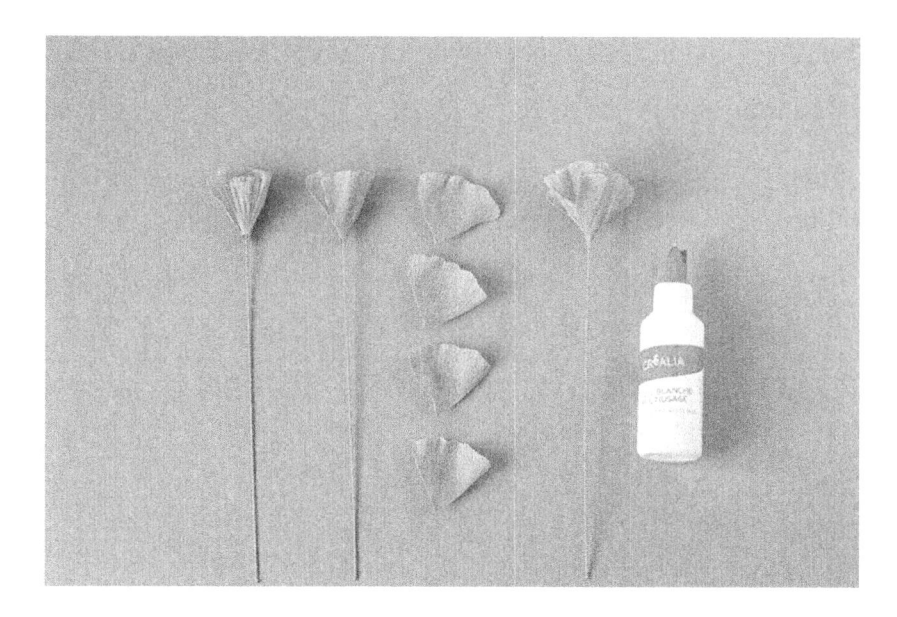

Glue the second petal offset by about 5 millimeters. Glue by wrapping the first 7 petals to surround the flower several times. Pinch the base to refine it.

Glue the second set of heart- shaped petals onto the flower.

Glue each petal a little higher than the base, on the first petals to create a more garnished effect .

Paste wrapping around the petals of the flower.

Finish by gluing the last set of 6 rounded petals, arranging to surround the flower only once.

Turn the flower over and glue the sepals starting from the stem to cover the base of the flower.

Cut a strip of green crepe paper about 0.4 x 15 cm long .

Shoot it. Glue it to the base of the sepals.

Apply glue and wrap it tightly around the rod. Let dry.

Prepare 5 hot pink peonies and 4 soft pink peonies in this way.

The foliage

Print the template and cut it out using Cricut. Cut 10 leaves from green florist crepe paper. Be sure to place the vertical template in the direction of the grooves of the crepe paper. Cut a wire to be tied in half using wire cutters. Paste the wire bonding at the center of the foliage. Cut a strip of green crepe paper about 0.4 x 15 cm long. Shoot it. The paste to the base of the foliage. Apply glue and wrap it tightly around the rod. Let dry. Prepare 10 green leaves in this way.

17 Floral Letter In Watercolor

Time: 60 minutes

Material

- Cricut Maker
- Box of 12 Aqua pencils
- 3 watercolor brushes
- Watercolor pad 25 x 25 cm
- 200 Double-sided adhesive foam squares - Créalia
- Extra strong double-sided adhesive tape - 6mm x 10m - Créalia
- Template to download and print.

Directions

Print the templates and using the tracing paper, reproduce the letter chosen on the watercolor paper as well as the flowers.

Color the letter with watercolor pencils. Make areas darker to create contrast

Apply water to the entire letter with a watercolor brush

Color the plants. For flowers, put different colors on the petals

With the watercolor brush, apply water and blend the colors together

For the foliage, apply a first color and add lines of different colors to create nuances

Cut out the patterns using Cricut maker.

Glue the patterns on the letter using the foam squares. Then glue everything on the canvas with double-sided tape.

Your floral monogram is ready.

18 Paper Fans

Materials

- Circuit Maker
- A4 papers
- Round scalloped perforator 7.5 cm
- Punch Round 3.8cm
- Double-sided
- Mini high temperature glue gun

Instructions

1. Fold a sheet of A4 paper accordion lengthwise in Cricut maker. Repeat for 2 more sheets of paper.
2. Fold the accordions in half in the middle.
3. Add double-sided tape to the ends

4. Secure the parts together. You must have 3 identical parts.

5. Glue the 3 parts together with double-sided tape to form the pennant.

6. Cut circles using circuit from colored or patterned paper using a scalloped circle hole punch.

7. Glue the circles in the center of each pennant using the glue gun.

8. Repeat the operation with a smaller round hole punch. You can create larger diameter flags by gluing 2 A4 sheets together in the longest part of the paper beforehand to form A3 paper.

9. Create several fans by varying sizes to decorate your party atmosphere.

19 Thankyou Box

Materials

- The Cricut Machine
- Color papers
- Glue
- Removable golden vinyl
- Gold Marker
- The template
- The typos used are Courrier new and Adalaide (the latter is from Cricut)
- For those who can log into Cricut, here is the Design Space project link .

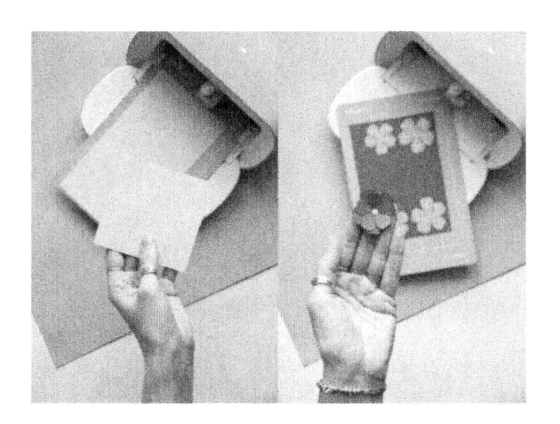

Instructions

- Using your application prepare the cutting of your paper templates for your box, as well as the paper decorations (ex: leaves / flowers / hearts).

- Prepare the cutting of your heart stickers with your SMART VINYL REMOVABLE Gold paper which you will use to close your box.

- Now that the paper templates are cut out, use your GOLD marker to create and draw your texts. You can choose to write whatever you want.

It's time to stick your papers on your cardboard box. The "Thank you" paper is to be placed inside the box on the upper part. Also place your plain pink paper template at the bottom of your box.

Now stick your paper with your text "Just for you" on the outside of the box.

Come and create your floral arrangement inside your box using strong glue, I decided to add a real craspedia to it so that I don't just have paper. If not, you can add a branch of eucalyptus, or olive tree.

Once your interior decoration is finished, you can now close your box and seal it with your golden heart stickers. All you have to do is offer them.

CHAPTER 5:

Projects For Connoisseurs Or "Intermediate"

Let's start these projects using fabric as the base material. You will learn to create a variety of projects that you can further customize as you follow the instructions below and have unique designs of your own.

20 Fabric Headband

Materials

- "Cricut Maker" or "Cricut Explore"

- Fabric grip mat, gray polka dot fabric, and thread, black or decorative elastic, home sewing machine.

Instructions

1. Log into the "Design Space" application and click on the "New Project" button on the top right corner of the screen to view a blank canvas.

2. Click on the "Projects" icon and type in "fabric headband" in the search bar.

3. Click on "Customize" to further edit the project to your preference or simply click on the "Make It" button and load the fabric to your "Cricut" machine by placing the right side down on the mat and follow the instructions on the screen to cut your project.

4. For assembly, measure your head where you would wear the headband and minus 15 inches from the measurement then cut the elastic at that length to use underneath the headband.

5. Place the right sides together and pin the elastic inside with the ends sticking out that can be pinned at the end of the headband.

6. Use the sewing machine sew around the outside edge of the headband, leaving 0.5-inch seam. Then sew over the ends of the elastic while it is between the two headband pieces leaving 2 inches opening unsewn along one side of the headband.

7. Clip around the seam allowances with snips and turn the headband right side out. Use the end of a spoon to turn the edges of the headband out, then use an iron to press and solidify the shape.

8. Top stich around the edge of the headband with a quarter-inch seam allowance for a finished look and close the turning hole.

21 Forever Fabric Banner

Materials

- "Cricut Maker" or "Cricut Explore"

- fabric grip mat

- glitter iron-on (black, pink)

- "Cricut EasyPress," weeder

- pink ribbon, canvas fabric

- sewable fabric stabilizer

- sewing machine and thread

Instructions

- Log into the "Design Space" application and click on the "New Project" button on the top right corner of the screen to view a blank canvas.

- Click on the "Projects" icon and type in "fabric banner" in the search bar.

- Click on "Customize" to further edit the project to your preference or simply click on the "Make It" button. Place the trimmed fabric on the cutting mat removing the paper backing, then load it to your "Cricut" machine and follow the instructions on the screen to cut your project. Similarly, load the iron-on vinyl sheet to the "Cricut" and cut the design, making sure to mirror the image.

- Carefully remove the excess material from the sheet using the "weeder tool," making sure only the design remains on the clear liner.

- Using the "Cricut EasyPress Mini" and "EasyPress Mat" the iron-on layers can be easily transferred to the fabric. Preheat your "EasyPress Mini" and put your iron-on vinyl design on the fabric and apply pressure for a couple of minutes or more. Wait for a few minutes prior to peeling off the design while it is still warm.

22 Fabric Flower Brooch

Materials

- "Cricut Maker" or "Cricut Explore"
- fabric grip mat
- printable iron-on
- "Cricut EasyPress"
- Weeder
- fabric pencil pouch
- Inkjet printer

Instructions

- Log into the "Design Space" application and click on the "New Project" button on the top right corner of the screen to view a blank canvas.

- Click on the "Projects" icon and type in "fabric pouch" in the search bar.

- Click on "Customize" to further edit the project to your preference or simply click on the "Make It" button and follow the prompts on the screen for using ink jet printer to print the design on your printable vinyl and subsequently cut the design.

- Carefully remove the excess material from the sheet using the "weeder tool," making sure only the design remains on the clear liner.

- Using the "Cricut EasyPress Mini" and "EasyPress Mat" the iron-on layers can be easily transferred to the fabric. Preheat your "EasyPress Mini" and put your iron-on vinyl design on the fabric and apply pressure for a couple of minutes or more. Wait for a few minutes prior to peeling off the design while it is still warm.

23 Leather Flower Hat

Materials

- "Cricut Maker" or "Cricut Explore,"
- standard grip mat
- Cricut Faux Leather
- button, strong adhesive
- hat

Instructions

1. Log into the "Design Space" application and click on the "New Project" button on the top right corner of the screen to view a blank canvas.

2. Click on the "Projects" icon and type in "leather flower hat" in the search bar.

3. Click on "Customize" to further edit the project to your preference or simply click on the "Make It" button and load the faux leather to your "Cricut" machine by placing it face down on the mat and follow the instructions on the screen to cut your project.

4. For assembly, glue tabs on each flower together to give shape to every single layer and let dry.

5. Glue all the flower layers on top of one another with the biggest layer at the bottom. Once the flower dries completely, glue button on the center of the flower. And finally, glue the flower to the hat.

24 Floral Mousepad

Materials

- "Cricut Maker" or "Cricut Explore"
- fabric grip mat
- printable fabric
- mousepad
- adhesive

Instructions

1. Log into the "Design Space" application and click on the "New Project" button on the top right corner of the screen to view a blank canvas.

2. Click on the "Images" icon on the "Design Panel" and type in "#MB145E" in the search bar. Select the image and click on the "Insert Images" button at the bottom of the screen.

3. Edit the project to your preference or simply click on the "Make It" button and load the vinyl sheet to your "Cricut" machine and follow the instructions on the screen to print and cut your project.

4. Once you have the printed fabric cut, use the adhesive to adhere it to the mousepad.

25 Jelly Bean Burp Cloth

Materials

- "Cricut Maker" or "Cricut Explore"
- fabric grip mat, fabric
- (light gray, teal)
- rotary cutter
- turning tool
- sewing machine
- thread

Instructions

1. Log into the "Design Space" application and click on the "New Project" button on the top right corner of the screen to view a blank canvas.

2. Click on the "Projects" icon and type in "jelly bean burp cloth" in the search bar.

3. Click on "Customize" to further edit the project to your preference or simply click on the "Make It" button. Place the trimmed fabric on the cutting mat then load it to your "Cricut" machine and follow the instructions on the screen

to cut your project. (Pay attention to the direction of the print for each fabric piece).

4. With the right sides together, pin the two bean pieces together and sew with a 6mm seam around the edge of the bean pieces, leaving a 1-2 inch opening for turning in the middle straight area.

5. Clip all curves generously and use a chopstick to turn the fabric pieces' right side out through the turning hole. Press all seams.

6. Lastly, top stitch the entire shape and close the turning hole as well.

26 Personalized Coaster Tiles

Materials

- "Cricut Maker" or "Cricut Explore"
- standard grip mat
- "Cricut" iron-on lite
- freezer paper
- "Cricut EasyPress Mini"
- "EasyPress" mat
- weeding tool
- pillow cover
- screen print paint
- paintbrush

Instructions

1. Log into the "Design Space" application and click on the "New Project" button on the top right corner of the screen to view a blank canvas.

2. Click on the "Images" icon on the "Design Panel" and type in "#MED91E0" in the search bar. Select the image and

click on the "Insert Images" button at the bottom of the screen.

3. Edit the project to your preference or simply click on the "Make It" button and load the freezer paper with the non-shiny side up on the mat to your "Cricut" machine and follow the instructions on the screen to cut your project.

4. Using a weeder tool, remove the negative space pieces of the design. Carefully place the stenciled quote on the pillow.

5. Using the "Cricut EasyPress Mini" and "EasyPress Mat", iron on the design to the pillow. Preheat your "EasyPress Mini" and put your design on the desired area and apply pressure for couple of minutes or more. Remove the freezer paper and let it dry overnight.

6. Set the paint with the "EasyPress" once again and enjoy your new pillow!

CHAPTER 6:

Projects For Experts

27 Personalized Mugs (Iron-On Vinyl)

Materials

- Cricut Maker or Cricut Explore

- Standard Grip mat

- Printable Cricut iron-on, or heat transfer vinyl

- Cricut Easy Press Mini

- Easy Press mat

- Weeding tool

- Ceramic mug

Instructions

- Log into the **'Design Space'** application and click on the **'New Project'** button on the top right corner of the screen to view a blank canvas.

- Click on the **'Images'** icon on the **'Design Panel'** and type in **'America'** in the search bar. Click on the desired image, then click on the **'Insert Images'** button at the bottom of the screen.

- Click on **'Templates'** icon on the **'Designs Panel'** located on the left of the screen, and type in **'Mug'** in the templates search bar, and select the mug icon.

- You can change the **'Type'** and **'Size'** of the template to decorate mugs with non-standard sizes by clicking on the **'Size'** icon, and selecting **'Custom'** to update your mug size.

- You can further edit your design by clicking on the **'Shapes'** icon adding: hearts, stars or other desired shapes to your design.

- Click on **'Save'** at the top right corner of the screen and give desired name to the project, for example, **'Mug Decoration'** and click **'Save'**.

- The design is ready to be printed and cut. Simply click on the **'Make It'** button, and follow the prompts on the screen for using the ink jet printer to print the design on your printable iron-on vinyl, and subsequently, cut the design.

- Carefully remove the excess material from the sheet using the '**Weeder Tool**', making sure only the design remains on the clear liner.

- Using the '**Cricut Easy Press Mini**' and '**Easy Press Mat**' the iron-on layers can be easily transferred to your mug. Preheat your '**Easy Press Mini**' and put your design on the desired area and apply pressure for a couple of minutes, or more (Sample project in the picture below). Wait for few minutes prior to peeling off the design, while it is still warm. (Since the design is delicate, use the spatula tool, or your fingers to rub the letters down the mug before starting to peel the design).

28 Personalized Coaster Tiles

Materials

- Cricut Maker, or Cricut Explore

- Standard grip mat

- Printable Cricut iron-on, or heat transfer vinyl

- Cricut Easy Press Mini Easy Press mat

- Weeding tool

- Ceramic coaster tiles

Instructions

- Log into the Design Space application, and click on the **'New Project'** button on the top right corner of the screen to view a blank canvas.

- Let us use our own image for this project. Search the web to find a monogram image that you would like and store it on your computer.

- Now, click on **'Upload'** icon from the **'Designer Panel'** on the left of the screen.

- A screen with **'Upload Image'** and **'Upload Pattern'** will be displayed.

- Click on the **'Upload Image'** button. Click on **'Browse'**, or simply drag and drop your image on the screen.

- Select the image type **'Simple'** and save the image as a **'Print Then Cut Image'**.

- Choose the uploaded image by clicking on the **'Insert Images'** and edit the image as needed.

- You can personalize the monogram by adding text to the design by clicking on the **'Text'** icon and typing in **'Your Name'**, or any other phrase.

- For the image below, the font **'American Uncial Corn Regular'** in regular and color (green) were selected.

- Select the text and the image and click on **'Group'**, then copy-paste your design for as many times as needed and save the project.

- You can resize the design as needed, to match the size of your coaster, although the recommended size is 4 x 4 inches for most common tile coasters. The design is ready to be printed and cut. Simply click on the **'Make It'** button and follow the prompts on the screen for using ink jet printer to print the design on your printable iron-on vinyl, and subsequently cut the design.

- Carefully remove the excess material from the sheet using the **'Weeder Tool'**, making sure only the design remains on the clear liner.

- Using the **'Cricut Easy Press Mini'** and **'Easy Press Mat'**, the iron-on layers can be easily transferred to your mug.

- Preheat your **'Easy Press Mini'** and put your design on the desired area, and apply pressure for couple of minutes or more. Wait for few minutes prior to peeling off the design while it is still warm.

29 Vinyl Chalkboard

Materials

- Cricut Maker or Cricut Explore

- Standard Grip mat

- Cricut Linen vinyl in desired colors

- Weeder, transfer tape

- Chalkboard and chalk pen

Instructions

- Log into the **'Design Space'** application and click on the **'New Project'** button on the top right corner of the screen to view a blank canvas.

- Click on the **'Projects'** icon and type in **'Vinyl Chalkboard'** in the search bar.

- Click on **'Customize'** to further edit the project to your preference, or simply click on the **'Make It'** button and load the vinyl sheet to your Cricut machine, and follow the instructions on the screen to cut your project.

- Using a Weeder tool, remove the negative space pieces of the design.

- Use the transfer tape to apply the vinyl cuts to the chalkboard. Then use the scraper tool on top of the transfer tape to remove any bubbles, and then just peel off the transfer tape.

- Lastly, use chalk pen to write messages.

30 Glitter Tumbler

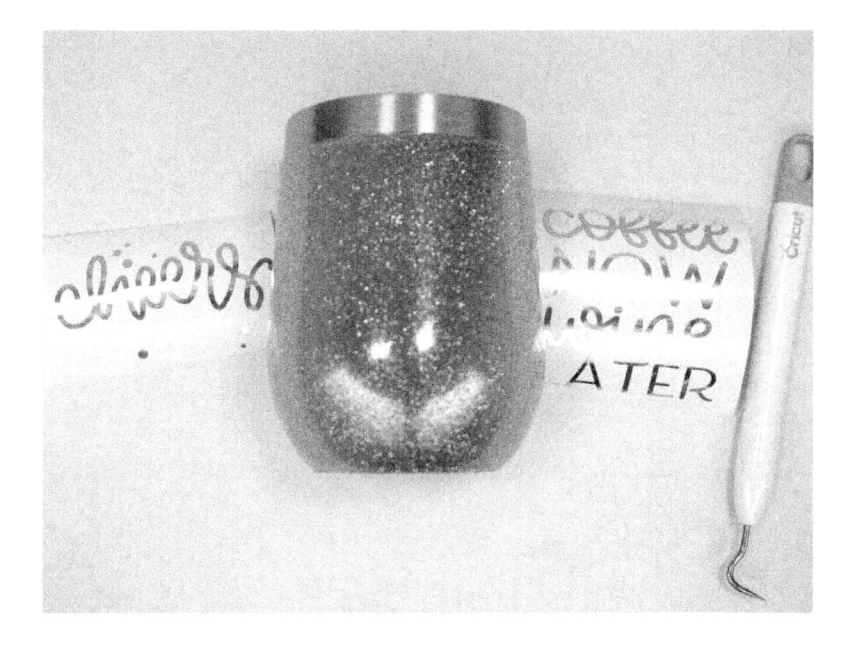

Materials

- Painters tape

- Mod podge and paint brush

- Epoxy

- Glitter

- Stainless steel tumbler

- Spray paint

- Vinyl

- Sandpaper wet/dry

- Gloves
- Plastic cup
- Measuring cup
- Rubbing alcohol

Instructions

- Tape off the top, and bottom of the tumbler.
- Make sure to seal them well enough that paint will not get on either side.
- Spray paint twelve inches away from your tumbler, in an area that is well ventilated.
- Make sure that the items you used are approved, and will not make you sick.
- Once your tumbler is dry from the paint you have used, you can add the glitter.
- This will make a mess, so have something under it to catch the glitter.
- Put the mod podge in a small container.
- Use a flat paintbrush to put it on.
- Take the lid off, and rotate the cup adding glitter gradually.

- Make sure it is completely covered.

- Make sure that an excess glitter will come off before removing the tape, and letting it dry.

- When dry, take a flat brush that is clean, and stroke down the glitter to get any additional pieces not glued down.

- Add a piece of tape above glitter line.

- Do the same to the bottom.

- Get a plastic cup and gloves.

- Use the epoxy, and measure equal parts of solution A and B into measuring cups. If it is a small mug you only need about 15 ml each. Larger ones need 20 ml.

- Pour them both in a cup, and scrape down the sides using a wooden stick.

- Stir for three minutes and pop all bubbles.

- Your gloves should be on, but if not; put them on now.

- Add the glitter to the epoxy and stir.

- Add the mixture to the tumbler, and turn it often while you are doing this. Having a roller or something to turn it on, will help and make sure it is in the air so nothing is touching it.

- When the drugs are not coming as fast you can, slow the turning down but make sure the turning is constant.

- Take the tape off after forty-five minutes.

- Spin the tumbler for five hours; it should be dry, if not, leave it on a foam roller overnight.

- Sand the tumbler gently with wet sandpaper.

- When it is all smooth from sanding, clean it with rubbing alcohol.

- Then open Cricut design space, and cut out your glitter vinyl.

- Weed the design.

- Add a strong grip transfer tape.

- Transfer the decal to the tumbler.

This is a very hard project that takes a lot of time, and you need to make sure that children are nowhere near these products as it will be fatal to them, if they swallow them. Another thing to remember is spinning and making sure it is dry. By following these instructions, you should have a great glitter tumbler that you can take anywhere, and rock a stylish look. This is a great idea for business owners as well because decorated tumblers are a hot commodity right now, and everyone loves them.

31 Personalized Mermaid Bottle

Materials

- You will need a water bottle with a smooth surface (these are very easy to find in dollar stores, superstores, specialty stores or really any store you would like to go into)

- Transfer tape

- A brayer, or a scraper

- Outdoor vinyl

Instructions

1. Your first step is to open the Design app. Let us say for this example, we are going to be making a mermaid.

2. Choose a font that you like, and then use the eyeball icon in the layers panel. If you do not want to make it yourself, simply go into the design space and choose one of their ready to make projects.

3. Create a second text box so you can make the picture bigger.

4. Now you will need to attach the two layers together so that the picture cut, and the initial cut, are joined together.

5. Resize and make it fit your water bottle.

6. To make sure that this will adhere to your bottle, you will need to use transfer tape. The brayer can help here because you can help press the transfer tape down.

7. Start in the center of the letter, and work out when adhering to the bottle. Be sure to smooth all bubbles.

8. Peel off the tape very carefully, and then you are finished.

To make the shark follow these directions:

1. Your first step is to open the Design app. This time we are making the shark.

2. Choose a font that you like, and then use the eyeball icon in the layers panel. If you do not want to make it yourself

simply go into the design space, and choose one of their ready to make projects.

3. Create a second text box so you can make the picture bigger.

4. Now you will need to attach the two layers together, so that the picture cut and the initial cut together.

5. Resize to make it fit your water bottle.

6. To make sure that this will adhere to your bottle, you will need to use transfer tape. The brayer can help here because you can help press the transfer tape down.

7. Start in the center of the letter and work out when adhering to the bottle. Be sure to smooth all bubbles.

8. Peel off the tape very carefully and then you are finished.

By utilizing the tips in this chapter, you will be able to make some great projects, and really get used to your machine and its inner workings, as well as unleash your own creativity and learn. The Cricut machines have made crafting so much easier, and a lot more fun. The fact that Cricut also works with many companies in order for you to be able to use their designs, makes this perfect for fans of pop culture.

Enjoy taking your crafting skills to the next level and learning great new projects with the Cricut machines!

32 Gift Wrap

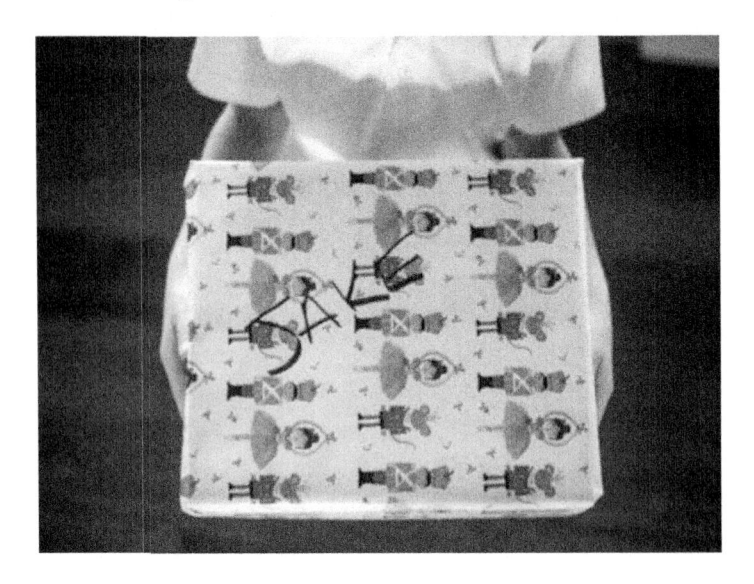

Materials

- Cricut machine (either series)
- Cricut pens (you choose the color)
- 12" x 24" mat
- White Kraft paper

Instructions

- Open the Design Space and select the design.
- **'Duplicate'** the images until you have what you need, and then resize and rotate them until you are happy with how it looks.

- When you have a 12" x 12" section, you can hit CTRL+A to select all of it and copy and paste the design below. It will save a lot of work.

- **'Attach'** the whole design to keep it all together.

- **'Select All'** again and check your measurements before sending the design to your machine.

- **Hit** 'Make It'.

- The machine may remind you that you need a bigger mat.

- Wait until it is finished. Once it is done be careful removing it from your mat, and then you can wrap your gifts.

CHAPTER 7:

Special Occasion Projects

33 Halloween Spiders

Materials

- SVG Spider web file
- Cricut machine
- Adhesive
- Black paper
- Pieces of parchment paper

Instructions

- Place the SVG file into the Design Space and proceed to cut into different web sizes.

- Place the parchment papers on the work area.

- Arrange the spider web just how you want it to look on the worktable.

- After the arrangement of the web, move onto joining the edges of the webs with your adhesive. You have to be careful here to make sure that you get only the edges joined together.

- Wait for a few minutes to get it properly dried.

- Hang it around the house, and you have your perfect Halloween Spider web design!

34 3-in-1 Winter Crafts Snowflake

While you can make an assortment of event ventures with this cut archive, this guide will tell you the best way to make a fast card and token decoration. You can change the hues and materials to accommodate your own style.

Materials

- Cricut Maker cutting machine and Cricut Access
- Snowflake SVG record
- Light blue felt
- Holographic iron-on vinyl
- White sparkle iron-on vinyl
- Twine
- Iron or EasyPress

Instructions

To begin with, we should make the decoration/blessing tag.

- Resize this design to 3" wide, ungroup the layers and disguise all the draw lines.

- Set the establishment layer for the blue felt.

- Set the point by point top layer design for holographic iron-on.

- Set the leaf shape subtleties for white sparkle iron-on vinyl.

- Adhere to on-screen guidelines to cut the various layers.

- Cut a touch of twine at any rate 10" long. Spot twine on the blue felt near the highest point of one of the snowflake arms.

- Iron-on, the holographic iron-on vinyl, guaranteeing the twine is between the felt and the vinyl when you press it.

- Iron the white sparkle vinyl set up.

- Knot the twine into a little bow at the highest point of the snowflake. Tie a knot toward the completion of the twine to make an adjusting circle for your trimming or blessing tag.

How about we make the card.

- Cut out a little card and envelope set.

- Cut a touch of silver sparkle vinyl to fit the front of the card. Recognize the vinyl on the facade of the card.

- Utilizing a hole punch or instrument, poke an opening in the front of the card.

- Spot the adornment on the facade of the card and verify it into place by getting the twine tie through the card hole and tape set up inside the card.

35 Spiderweb Garland

Regardless of whether you need to make a Halloween wreath for your shelf or a fun complement to a whole staircase railing, you can make a custom expressive topic piece effectively. You simply cut out as many various spiderweb pieces as you require and interface them with a stick. You can likewise utilize this spiderweb pattern to make party welcome signs, shirt designs with shimmer vinyl, or make a custom divider workmanship design.

Materials

- Cricut Machine
- Cricut Design Space™ programming

- Spiderweb Garland Make-it-Now venture designed by Jen Goode

- 12" x 12" StandardGripCricut® tangle

- Black cardstock

- Adhesive

Instructions

- Slice design holding fast to on-screen guidelines group changes

- Paste spiderweb out, as demonstrated by the format — allow to dry.

- Show as wanted.

Tip: Don't worry over dried glue appearing on your completed piece, you can flip the whole web over so the glue is on the back.

36 Christmas Ornament

Materials

- Cricut machine

- Cricut glitter vinyl

- Transfer tape

- Scraper tool

- Weeding tool

- Ribbon

- Ornaments

Instructions

- Log in to the Cricut design space and start a new project.
- Click on the Input icon.
- Type in your Christmas greetings.
- Change the text font.
- Ungroup and adjust the spacing.
- Highlight and "weld" to design the overlapping letters.
- Select the parts of the text you do not want as part of the final cut.
- Readjust the text size.
- Select the file as a cut file. You will get to preview the design as a cut file.
- Approve the cut file.
- The text is ready to cut.
- Place the vinyl on the cutting mat shiny side down.
- Load the mat into the machine.
- Custom dial to vinyl.
- Cut the image.

- Use the weeding tool to remove excess vinyl after the image is cut.

- Apply a layer of transfer tape to the top of the cut vinyl.

- Peel back the vinyl paperback.

- Apply the vinyl onto the glass ornament.

- Go over the applied vinyl with a scraper tool to remove air bubble underneath the vinyl.

- Slowly peel away the transfer tape from the glass ornament.

37 Wedding Invitation

Materials

- "Cricut" cutting machine
- cutting mat
- cardstock or your choice of decorative paper/crepe paper/fabric
- home printer (if not using "Cricut Maker")

Instructions

- Use your "Cricut ID" to log in to the "Design Space" application. Then click on the "New Project" button on the top right corner of the screen to start a new project and view a blank canvas.

- A beginner-friendly way to create wedding invitations is a customization of an already existing project form the "Design Space" library that aligns with your own ideas. Click on the "Projects" icon on the "Design Panel" then select "Cards" from the "All Categories" drop-down. Enter the keywords "wedding invite" in the search bar.

- You can click on the project to preview its description and requirements. Once you have found the project you want to use, click "Customize" at the bottom of the screen, so you can edit the invite and add the required text to it.

- The design will be loaded on to the canvas. Click on the "Text" button and type in the details for your invite. You will be able to modify the font, color as well as the alignment of the text from the "Edit Text Bar" on top of the screen. You can even adjust the size of the entire design as needed. (An invitation card can be anywhere from 6 to 9 inches wide)

- Note – Most cards will require you to change the "Fill" to "Print" on the top of the screen so you can first print then cut the invitation.

- Select the entire design and click on the "Group" icon on the top right of the screen under "Layers Panel." Then click on the "Save" button to enter a name for your project and click "Save" again.

- Your design can now be printed then cut. Simply click on the "Make It" button on the top right corner of the screen to view the required mats and material. Then use your home printer to print the design on your chosen material (white cardstock or paper), or if using the "Cricut Maker," then just follow the prompts on the "Design Space" application.

Tip: Calibrate your machine first for the "Print then Cut" project by clicking on the hamburger icon following to the "Canvas" ≡ Canvas on the top left of the screen and follow the prompts on the screen, as shown in the picture below.

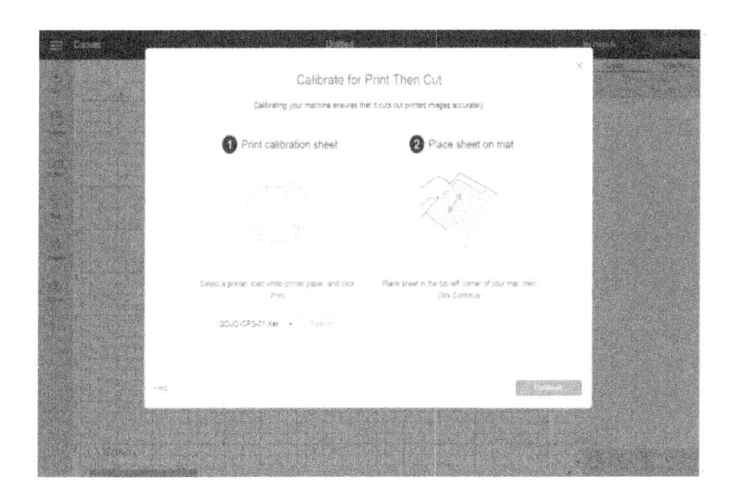

- Load the material with printed design to your "Cricut" cutting machine and click "Continue" at the bottom right corner of the screen to start cutting your design.

- Once you're "Cricut" device has been connected to your computer, set the cut setting to "cardstock." Then place the printed cardstock on top of the cutting mat and load into the "Cricut" device by pushing against the rollers.. Viola! You have your wedding invitations all ready to be put in an envelope and on their way to all your wedding guests.

CHAPTER 8:

How To Sell Your Project Online

Before you start trying to make money from your Cricut, take some time to think about whether or not it really is what you want to do.

When I bought Cricut, I thought about starting a personalization and stationery business, but everything in life is trial and error, I am still in the testing phase.

Here are some things to think about before "launching":

- Are you doing it just because your friends say your creations are amazing?

- Do you want to support your family financially?

- Are you doing it for some extra money?

- Are you willing to deal with HARD customers? (there are always difficult clients)

- Do you want to turn your hobby into a job?

- Can you learn more about marketing on and off the network?

- Do you have enough time and space to start a small business?

- Do you like to make crafts with your Cricut? So much to do over and over again?

I definitely don't want to discourage you from starting to make money from your Cricut, but you have to put your feet on the ground and I also want you to **be smart about it**.

Your answers to these questions do not necessarily determine your decision whether to launch or not, BUT they will help you realize what it will be like for you to start a small business with your Cricut.

All About Copyright

Since you decided to get into this business, we should talk about licenses and copyrights, as this is the area where you can get into trouble the fastest.

And the question why ?, because all the images, cut files that you download or even copies from the

Internet were created by someone, and the simple fact of finding them on Google does not give you the right to reproduce it or worse, sell it on the Internet.

There are different policies that protect images, below I describe the most common.

Cricut Angel Policy

Within the same Cricut Design Space system there is a library of Cricut images to create with the machine. You can create and sell with such designs but under the "Cricut Angel" Policy . Please read this policy carefully , you will find many things there, Some things it mentions:

- Most Cricut Access images are included in this policy.

- Create up to 10,000 items to sell using Cricut images.

- Don't just sell individual images.

- You must include a copyright notice with your projects.

- Do not include licensed content, such as images from Disney or Marvel.

Personal Use Vs. Commercial Use

If you prefer to use very specific images, you can buy them in online stores. Don't just download them from Google images and put them in your projects... It is very likely that if you do, you are violating copyrights. When purchasing images online, be sure to read the file's terms of use. Most of these images only include a personal use license, that is, you cannot create products to sell with these types of files. There may also be the option to buy the same image but with a commercial license, just remember to read the terms.

There are images of licensed characters that normally belong to Disney and / or Marvel, such as (and this will surprise you as much as I do): Elsa from Frozen or Iron Man from Marvel. Using these images is breaking copyright and you may have trouble using it as a way to make money. My advice would be to stay away from using these images, it can bring you an ugly problem and even a lawsuit or fine.

Starting A Cricut Craft Business

Now that we are clear on the Legal topic, let's talk about how to earn money and get the best out of your Cricut.

Define Your Niche

One of the worst things you can do is do whatever people ask you to do. A glass here, a personalization over there, a cake topper from today to tomorrow.

You'll end up with lower margins than the market, perhaps wasted product and a confused audience.

I recommend defining your niche and type of product to one or very few elements and / or themes so that you can have a strong and your audience can remember you faster.

When deciding what type of products to sell, consider "added value." This can be additional things to your product or just perfect it. In this way you could charge a "premium" price.

Buy Materials In Large Quantities

Having decided on your niche, you can buy your supplies and materials, what I call "wholesale". This is nothing more than buying large quantities, say 10 foot vinyl rolls, boxes of 10 glasses or cups at cheaper prices than if you buy them per unit. Cricut also sells wholesale materials.

Quality Really Matters

One of the fastest ways to destroy your business is to produce a low-quality product. Word of mouth travels faster than we think, and the worst part is that you can't change the ratings you get if you're selling your product in an online store. Therefore, when you are creating your business, make sure you can consistently produce quality products. If you understand that your quality is falling because you are not in control because you receive many requests, consider seeking help or stopping your orders for a short time.

Whatever you do, do it well.

How To Set The Price

It bothers me to see people selling their beautiful super elaborate creations at SO cheap prices. Those people are not even valuing their own time. They are not taking into account your talent, materials or many other things that are important when setting prices.

Monetizing Your Art

You have practiced, perfected and established a style of that art that you like to do so much. You have decorated cards, personalized objects, created pictures with motivational phrases; and with pride you have shared your work on social networks. Now comes the question that scares you so much. "What would you charge to do THIS?" It is super exciting and flattering to know that there are people who ask you to do what you love to earn money.

However, as exciting as it is, it scares us, and a LOT. To be honest I still feel nervous when sending a quote to my clients. We have all been there on several occasions, and I know it is difficult at first, but the most important thing is to have everything in order. Before you start thinking about monetizing your art, you should realize all the factors that you may not have considered when valuing your work. Believe it or not, there are many more reasons behind the prices, apart from "because that is what so-and-so charges." Alright then let's get started.

Someone Wants To Hire Me .. What Do I Do Now?

Congratulations! You must be super excited, but before responding with a price, or worse, offering to do it for free , there is a lot to consider when evaluating your work, and I hope I'm covering a large part here.

Why is pricing so important? Shouldn't I feel good just by putting the price that I understand "correct"? Well, it is not wrong to ask yourself this question, however you must be sure that you are not bothering yourself, the client and other artists in the business.

When you are self-employed, you are in charge of the money you earn, so you want to do it right. It is important that you ask yourself these questions before setting a price.

- How much is your time and energy worth to you?
- How does your experience compare to others in the business?
- What are your material costs?
- What is the size of the project?
- What is the project deadline?
- Are you going to include shipping, or charge extra?
- Is this piece going to be original, or is the customer making and selling multiple copies?
- Does the client want you to convert the artwork into a digital format?
- Will you be creating the artwork in your own studio or on-site?
- What will be your minimum charge for small jobs?

Your Time + Energy

This is where the wellness factor comes in, where you need to think about how much your time is worth to you. It's worth a lot more than buying the cheapest combo at McDonald's, but there the questions come... Karissa, how much exactly? How do I find out It is difficult to answer the frank but there are certain guidelines that I can tell you that can help you.

The typical answer is that you put yourself a monthly salary with which you feel comfortable, I will speak in an imaginary way based on some local statistics of the Dominican Republic to speak with numbers and you can understand. Let's say (I made it up) that on average a monthly salary in my country is $ 15,000 Dominican pesos and this is the number with which you value your time and energy.

This number will be divided by 4.3, this number is established as the average of weeks in the year since there are months that have 30 days, another 31 and February with 28. Already starting to see the difference? Now try to use that math to calculate your own hourly rate.

Start with the monthly salary you feel comfortable with:

_____

Divide that number by 4.3 and put it here: _____

Now divide this other number by 44 (remember that this number may vary). So this result is your hourly rate that you will put here:

_____

Your Level Of Experience

You may have been practicing or creating for a week or a year before being asked about working for money. This is more about the quality of your work, rather than how long you've been at it. BUT EYE: It is not that you are going to compare with artists who have a level of professionalism for a long time, it is a matter of an objective perspective.

Is it clean? Is consistent? Do you have your own style? Do you feel confident in your work? Have you taken workshops or courses to ensure your techniques are correct?

Cost Of Materials

Are you using cheap store markers or artist quality paints? Do you use expensive papers and prepared inks? Are they special items you need? Do you have to order online that are specific to some part of the world or available near you?

The value increases with the quality of your tools and materials, as well as your knowledge of them. If you answer "What kind of paint do you have / do you use?" With a "I don't know ... I've had it for a long time and the label it has is no longer visible" or "a friend gave it to me and I don't know where it got it "Your work will not be as valuable as that of someone whose answer is" I use Winsor and Newton's lightweight, water-resistant watercolors. "

Artist-quality materials cost more, so it's important that you know the cost of your materials in case they run out.

Also, for a big job, you may have to burn seven special markers. That is a part of the cost that you do not want out of your time or pocket, but is an expense that must be included in your estimate.

Of course, if in a job you used only part of the material, obviously you are not going to charge the full cost of that material, there you must use mathematics, knowing in advance how much of the material you used and obtaining a percentage.

Project Size

This is probably one of the first factors to value your project. How big is it? Creating something, for example a lettering composition is an 8 ½ x 11 inch sheet with ten words will take much less time and less materials than those same ten words on an 8x10 foot board. You can have a price for measurements, let's say square inches or better use your hourly rate that we work above.

Delivery / Shipping

You must indicate in your budget if the delivery is included or is an extraordinary payment. That means you need to know where the piece is going. You may have to purchase parcel shipping quotes outside of your city based on the weight size and service you really need. I recommend that you investigate the rates of the shipping companies and thus have a standard shipping cost.

Original Or Continuous Use?

Will your client use your art once (like a wedding card), continuously (like a business card or blog), or multiple times (like a T-shirt to resell)? It is always a good idea to ask this question in advance. The answer will help you determine how valuable your artwork is to the customer. If it will be used continuously to promote or generate direct income for your client, the value increases.

Deliverables

What should you deliver to your customer as a finished product? An original art? Or is it digital? Both of them? What file formats? JPG, PNG, TIF, EPS, AI? Do you have experience digitizing, and do you have the best tools to do it? Spending time digitizing and preparing multiple files takes time and experience, and therefore should be priced accordingly. There are also those printed from digital art. Will you mail the file? In a memory? Digital start and then you delivered it printed? All this must be taken into account considering the time and effort it took to do it. NOTE: a digital job is even more expensive since it can be reproduced and using specialized programs requires previous experience and learning, which I suppose also cost you to acquire it.

Location (In Or Out Of Your Studio)

Your hourly rate will also largely depend on where you will be doing the work.

When you have the luxury of your own space you can perform several tasks at the same time, that is, you can be working on two projects at the same time. This makes it easy to access all of your supplies and materials. The most convenient way for you to work in your own place, at your own pace with everything you need at hand, you should not worry about traffic.

If the job requires you to be somewhere outside your study (let's say a restaurant for example), the value of your time will increase significantly. You will have to travel to and from the place (which needs to be included in your work time), carry all your materials with you and only commit to that work during the assigned hours. That also means that you will be in an uncontrolled environment, this includes distractions, noise and curious people. It can be a lot of fun working on site, and it can be a real headache.

Sometimes a combination of time in your studio and on-site works best. You can carry out all the designs and preparatory work in the studio, so that you are ready to carry out your duties once you arrive on site. This would be shown as two separate hourly rates in the quote, breaking down your activities, so your client knows how they are investing their money in you.

Project Term

Only you know what time is most comfortable for you to work. If not, I recommend measuring the time you take doing your work to have an estimate and also a space in case something unforeseen occurs. If a client comes out of nowhere with a crazy panic because they are the most important in the world, ALWAYS add a fee for speed, clarifying the time it takes you in normal time for similar works, and that you will make an exception for him / her. Normally these prices vary between 50% or 100% of the labor price.

It is best to avoid these types of jobs because you start to get used to the client, only accept these cases if it is strictly necessary.

Your Minimum Price

You have heard the expression "I am not going to get out of bed for less than 1,000 pesos per hour." That is what we have to calculate. What hourly rate makes the project worth your time, energy and experience, in addition to cover any expenses or wear and tear on your supplies?

If someone asks you to do a tiny job, like "write my name", you need to be prepared with your minimum load. Sure, you will not charge her a price per name on invitation (say $ 50) and she would leave it like that.

Taking into account the time it will take to contact so-and-so for details (style, color, size, delivery, etc.), the time required to assemble your materials and to prepare your work space (remove the dishes from the dining room table by example , and send or deliver the final piece, $ 50 is not close to cover your time, energy and materials.

If you are an adept of higher technical knowledge, then you can generate great benefits by providing either quality custom work, bulk offering or informative network. It is advisable to concentrate your efforts on one approach to start with. If you choose, for example, a custom work approach, you increase the chances to find potential customers looking for your products as they turn to a search engine like Google to find what they are looking for. Websites like Amazon Handmade or Etsy provide a good platform to allow to sell custom design services. Equally efficient is the launch of your site. This strategy is worth looking at. Selling online presents advantages such as low startup costs and access to the global market with access to millions of potential customers. Furthermore, online custom prices tend to be lower than those on the local market. However, access to the global market means that competition is stiff, pushing products to be competitively priced. Selling online requires certain knowledge in logistics as far as shipping and packing your products are concerned, a cost factor that needs to be taken into consideration in your pricing.

If the approach of bulk offering or volume sales is the one that you prefer, then the advantages are similar to reducing the cost per unit produced. eBay and Amazon have become the largest platforms. On the other hand, if an online retail business approach is more what you may be inclined to do, then this approach will give you the ability to determine the demand for the designs you offer and plan the production accordingly. But selling online means challenging the existing competition!

Finally, if you prefer to sell your products online through information network, then you can become an authority in the field, creating the opportunity to generate profit with your Cricut designs. By offering blogs on technical know-how or inspiration work, you become selective on the posts you want to take on.

Starting a new business requires foremost a business strategy, the foundation for your future success. Asking yourself who your potential customers would be, what kind of products you can sell them and how are the first steps of a future startup business.

Approaching Local Markets

You can explore the option of selling your products from 'business to business'. In this configuration, the volume of sales is as important as the size of the production. This is the most challenging balance to reach for a new Cricut based business. The advantage of obtaining contractual work means you can negotiate to buy a large quantity from vendors. However, such 'golden' opportunities are hard to find since such contracts are open to competition. Yet, as a new start-up business, you can present your products specifically tailored for business customers. A custom work approach offers positive aspects as businesses always look for originality and good products. By creating such a relationship, your business is likely to become a point of reference for future contacts, hence launching many opportunities for upselling. However, it is important to bear in mind that finding such niche is, hard as competition is very stiff!

Another approach to consider for selling your products is from 'business to customer'. In this model, though the volume of sales remains important, your objective is to present your products to retail customers willing to buy them. Creativity, imagination will be keys to your success, as well as what type of media and medium you want to work in (e.g. T-shirts, mugs). Equally important is a retail space you will need to choose to offer your items. Experiencing different locations and products is all part of the efforts of a new start-up business. Also, a custom work approach for local customers will present advantages since the startup cost are the lowest of all the different strategies described so far. However, as a new business in the field, starting can be difficult. Word of mouth can be your first step as well as producing good products at an affordable price.

CHAPTER 9:

Important Tips & Tricks to Know When You Want To Sell Your Own Creations

Personalized gifts are among the most well-known styles on Pinterest, and you can create incredible presents to market along with your Cricut vinyl machine (Cricut research, Cricut explore air two, Cricut maker). Now we have got a listing of amazing projects to get your creative juices flowing so that you may begin earning cash with Cricut!

Would You Market Cricut Layouts?

Yes! The Cricut angel policy permits you to sell around 10,000 layouts annually with discounts created with Provo craft solutions. There's definitely room for one to increase your company and sell layouts made using Cricut products. Just be certain that you read over the total angel policy to make certain you are working inside.

What Are the Most Lucrative Cricut Companies?

The most rewarding Cricut companies are people who provide unique products that people wish to purchase. Why waste your time creating products that nobody is considering? Rather spend your time in exploring your competitors. Learn what other crafting organizations are doing well and where they're making errors. This could enable you to locate a complete in your marketplace so you can create things with lesser competition.

Could I Sell Cricut Pictures On Etsy?

Yes! Don't forget to check out the angel policy (listed above). You can sell items utilizing non-licensed images in the Cricut library or you could design your own graphics using illustrator or photoshop. You can't sell accredited pictures...believe Disney, marvel comics, etc.. These pictures are very popular and you'll see Etsy stores selling these kinds of pictures, but these stores can be closed down or perhaps sued for selling accredited pictures.

What Can I Create To Market Using A Cricut Maker?

First let us consider the audience that you would like to function. You can create and market your Cricut designs to folks who wish to DIY their particular crafts or even you are able to create crafts to make and sell on Etsy, at craft fairs, and stalls.

If you choose to sell your designs it might be useful to know how to create SVG documents and use illustrator or photoshop. This may develop into a passive revenue choice, as you could set the files on the internet and people could immediately download them.

Making craft jobs to market is your next alternative. You can use online tutorials to make your own crafts. To be able to stick out from your opponent's you'll have to make items which are exceptional. This may mean using special materials, layouts, personalization's, or markets.

Side note: once I was exploring interesting Etsy stores. I found a store which produces "heterosexual women clothing " the dresses, dresses, skirts, and t-shirts from the store are made from prints which you typically find for boys. Matters like dinosaurs, rockets, science, robots, etc.. It is such an exceptional idea at a technical market for women who enjoy things which you don't typically find on women clothes.

You will find endless crafts to produce and sell using a Cricut machine. Can you know you could #monogram everything? (at least at the south????) Intelligent quotations, educator gifts, and even infant things can allow you to get your plastic company began. You are going to be earning money with Cricut shortly with those Cricut inspirations!

Private use vs. Industrial use

If you'd like additional pictures, you can get them from online stores. Don't just download pictures from google and utilize them to create jobs --you'll nearly definitely be violating copyright.

Should you purchase from online vendors, make certain to read the conditions of usage of this cut file! Most pictures you may buy include only a personal use license. You can't make items to market with documents which are only for private use.

You might have the choice to buy a commercial license. Some documents may come using a commercial permit. Again read the conditions!

Licensed Pictures

You might find pictures of characters that are licensed (believe Elsa out of frozen or iron man from marvel) on Etsy and at other stores. All these are usually breaking copyright and also you are able to get in trouble for using them. My advice? Stay away from accredited fonts and images!

And again, you cannot use accredited pictures from Cricut design space to market, though it's possible to use non-licensed pictures per their angel policy above.

Beginning A Cricut Craft Business

Alright, now that we have obtained that legal things out of the way, let us discuss the way to really make money with your Cricut!

Narrow Your Own Cricut Craft Niche

Among the worst things you can do is choose to simply make whatever folks ask one to create. A tumbler here, a house decor hint there, birthday t-shirts then. You are going to wind up with lower margins, wasted merchandise, along with a confused crowd.

Rather, narrow your product down to one or two things or topics and then nail it. I suggest choosing something in the junction of everything you love to create and what's rewarding (see below for pricing thoughts). That you wish to appreciate what you are creating --and you would like it to be worth your time.

When you are trying to decide what things to create and market along with your Cricut, think about "added value" this may include both enhancements to a product, or actually niching down. This way you may charge a premium for your goods.

A lot of people are making home-made hints, for example --possibly your "item" is adding paper succulents or hand-painted glitter accents. Perhaps you hand letter and flip your decoration into stickers for tops.

If you are making tumblers, perhaps they're specifically targeted to teachers and have a gift card holder. Perhaps your onesie store is filled with cute things especially for preemies.

If you are among the only people doing something, you are able to charge more! It also makes it much easier to target your advertisements, because you'll find below.

1 note--the bigger the item, the more difficult and more costly it is going to be to ship. You might choose to save those massive home decor hints for your regional craft fair.

Purchase Materials In Bulk

If you have nailed down your market, you can purchase your materials and supplies in bulk. You're able to purchase more tumblers or eyeglasses or vinyl at a more affordable price if you purchase in bulk. If you are still making "one off" items, it is far more difficult to keep in bulk.

If you are making holiday t-shirts, as an example, rather than purchasing routine rolls of iron vinyl in a craft shop, you can purchase in bulk to lower prices.

Conclusion

Well, there you have it! Everything you need to know about the Cricut Machine and Design Space software. This has been a very interesting trip into the world of the Cricut Machine and the various ways in which you can make it work wonders for you.

We have discussed how the Cricut Machine is a great tool for you to make your most imaginative and creative ideas come to life. Whether you are an avid hobbyist, or perhaps looking to take up a new craft, especially if you have some extra time on your hands, then the Cricut Machine offers various means for you to make your wildest ideas come to life.

So, what's the next step?

If you are still on the fence about purchasing your very own Cricut Machine, then it would be a great idea to do a cursory search online so you can get other users' impressions and opinions about this machine. By reading and hearing about what other users have to say, you can get an idea of just how useful this machine can be for you.

Also, do check out the various options in terms of models and pricing that are available to you. If you happen to be unsure about which model works best for you, take a minute to go back to the descriptions we have provided for each of the models. That way, if you are interested in a light machine that is good for less complex jobs, the Joy can work well for you. If you are looking for a heavy-duty machine, then the Maker is what you need. But if you are looking for the best all-around value, then the Explore Series can provide you with the features and functions you are looking for.

Additionally, do make a point of checking out blogs and social media where users and designers present their creations. Often, these blogs and social media sites can provide you with the inspiration you need to make your creations. Many times, it can be hard to tap into your creativity, especially when you don't have much experience with this type of machine. So, when you get ideas from other users, they can be a springboard to your magical creations.

In case you need a little extra help, Design Space Access has loads of ready-made projects from which you can choose. This is really useful when you are starting out and don't really have a sense of how the Cricut Machine works. Also, using ready-made projects can help you get a sense of how Design Space works and just how much you can do with it. Furthermore, bloggers and designers often share their project files. So, you can download them and then upload them to your Design Space account. Then, all you need is to cut, and away you go!

With that in mind, please take the time to go over any of the sections in this guide, which you feel can provide you with the insights that you need to make the best use of the Cricut Machine. The biggest step you can take is to make up your mind to get started with the Cricut Machine. Once you see how powerful it can be, you won't want to go without it.

Thank you for taking the time to go over this guide. If you have found it to be useful and informative, do tell others about it. In particular, those folks whom you meet in the Cricut community may need a helping hand. That's what this guide is all about.

Thanks again and happy cutting… or drawing, or coloring, or engraving… or scoring!

Printed in Great Britain
by Amazon